"John Blake has done a masterful job at putting the Christian life within reach of every new believer. John's book 'What Now God?' brings practical application to spiritual concepts and is a valuable tool for new believers. The simplicity of his presentation helps the new Christian put Biblical principals into 'shoe leather'. This book is a must for new Christians and is a vital resource for pastors and leaders in their discipleship strategies."

Tom Ferguson, D.D.
Foursquare N.W. District Supervisor

"Reading this practical guidebook, you will become more familiar with a God who not only invites us to know Him, but One who goes to such extraordinary lengths to reveal Himself. With precise and vivid strokes God is explained as the only one who can satisfy our deepest desires. As you read these pages and follow through with the exercises you will learn to cultivate that inner place where God wants to reign as Lord over every dimension of your life. I'm especially thankful that the book is so Christ centered, therefore so grace centered."

Dr. R. Allen Dunbar
President, Puget Sound Christian College
Member, Billy Graham Evangelical. Assocciation.

"John has presented a clear and concise introduction to Christianity. This book would be an excellent resource for those just beginning their journey with God. Church youth groups would profit much from this simple study of what it means to be saved. If you're an evangelist, here's the tool you've been looking for! Read it! Live it! Give it away!"

Peter Iliyn
YWAM North American Director

John has written a clear, kind, encouraging guide for people who are starting out on this walk of faith. I would definitely give it to people who have recently begun to follow Jesus. I particularly like the sections on the value of finding a loving, encouraging family of believers where we can all find the support we need as we try to figure out how to   follow Jesus in these confusing times.

Rev. Wes Johnson, ThM.
Pastor, Bethel Baptist Church, Everett, WA

"This is a wonderful book for new believers and Christians who have reached a plateau following Jesus Christ. Tools like this need to be multiplied."

David Livingston
Pastor for Cell Groups and Adult Ministries
Bethlehem Baptist Church, Minneapolis, MN

What Now, God?

ಜೆ

John S. Blake

Building the Foundation
for a Dynamic Christian Life

River City Press
Minneapolis, Minnesota

Scripture taken from the New King James Version
Copyright© 1982 by Thomas Nelson, Inc..
Used by permission. All rights reserved

Published by River City Press
4301 Emerson Avenue N.
Minneapolis, Minnesota 55412

Cover and layout design by Frontier Graphics
2221 Jade Avenue.
Everett, WA. 98201

Printed in the United States of America
ISBN 0-9706952-0-5

Library of Congress Cataloging-In-Publication Data
Blake, John S.
What Now God?: An introduction to Christian living
ISBN 0-9706952-0-5

For Sandy
The Love of My Life
୫୨୦୧

Contents

"If you abide in My word, you are My disciples indeed. And you shall know the truth, and the truth shall make you free."

(John 8:31-32)

Preface

There is an insatiable appetite for meaning within the life of every person. This hunger is so great that people of today resort to all kinds of unsatisfying attempts to quiet it. Many seek to quench their thirst and fill their hunger by accumulating things, only to find that possessions quickly lose their attraction. Drugs, easy sex and overdoses of endless entertainment reveal a profound longing in our culture. It all seems so ominous and bleak.

John Blake describes the "adventure" he and his wife Sandy have enjoyed as they also longed for meaning in their lives. I first met John because his journey of faith included fulfillment of the Degree Completion program at Puget Sound Christian College. His desire to help others find God as well as experience the deeper life of blessing that He offers through Jesus Christ shines from his life. That focus is carefully and clearly presented in the pages of this book.

Reading this practical guidebook, you will become more familiar with a God who not only invites us to know Him, but One who goes to such extraordinary lengths to reveal Himself. With precise and vivid strokes God is explained as the only one who can satisfy our deepest desires. As you read these pages and follow through with the exercises you will learn to cultivate that inner place where God wants to reign as Lord over every dimension of your life. I'm especially thankful that the book is so Christ-centered, therefore grace-centered.

So, on with the adventure! None of us are satisfied with

spiritual shallowness. Instead, we really can find balance as we experience Christ's presence for daily living.

Dr. R. Allen Dunbar
President, Puget Sound Christian College

The Prologue

You have no idea how important this book may be for you. You may read books with deeper insight, books with more information, even books which will have more impact on your life. But for you, at this moment in time, this may be the most important book you will read. In other cultures or another era, it wouldn't be so critical. But we live in the 21st century, where a new idea comes along every five minutes. Our attention span is similar to a gnat's, and our commitment level is about as deep as our attention span. So when the important things of life come our way, we have a difficult time recognizing what to do with them.

So here's the point: the idea of becoming a Christian, receiving the eternal life offered by Jesus, God's Son, is at a level of importance far beyond any other decision you will ever make in your life. Yet so many of us act as if it's no more significant than choosing the type of car we will drive. If that is so, what do you think will happen to your decision to follow Jesus, in a few days? I can tell you, because the statistics are already out there. *85% of all people who make a decision to become a Christian are not in church, or in any way practicing their faith three months later.* That's because they didn't realize the significance of their decision, they were caught up in the emotion of the moment, or they never took the time to become grounded and knowledgeable about the God they had chosen to serve. Soon, their initial excitement subsides and they are pulled away from God by the next glittery thing which the world offers. In the words of Jesus, the devil "snatches the truth away" and they go on as before. Nothing changes, except now they have been inoculated against hearing and believing the gospel again. Later times, when they hear again, the news of Christ's dying for their sins, their attitude will be, "Been there, done that. Didn't work."

Of course it didn't work! They never gave it a chance. Never really understood how much God loved them. Never heard about their inheritance in the Kingdom of God. Never spent any time finding out what this relationship with Jesus and His Father really meant.

That's what this book is about. It is meant to get you thoroughly grounded and informed about Christianity. It will explain the meaning of the sacrifice of Jesus. What He did. Why He did it. It will introduce you to the Father, Son and Holy Spirit, and their role in your new life as a child of God, a citizen of His Kingdom.

It will show you the fundamental scriptures which describe the basic truths of the gospel-scriptures which God handed down to us over the centuries. These are the timeless truths which we in our disposable society have simply tossed aside as if they were yesterday's news. This news is for all time! It has eternal significance, and for you, eternal value, if you receive it, believe it, and live by it. The tools of your future life are here in the pages of this book, for you to use if you choose.

Each chapter unfolds a vital area of information which will help and guide your journey. You will learn about the infinite love God has for you. You will find out how His love has resulted in a longing for relationship with you, and how you, in turn, have been created for relationship with Him. In that relationship, He has given you principles of life and guidelines which will bring fulfillment to your life, if you follow them. You will learn how you can have victory over temptations and bad habits. You will learn that each time you fall, God is there to pick you up, forgive you, and put you back on the right path. There is nothing you can do that God will not forgive, if you confess your sins and truly repent to him.

This book will also help you in your choice of a local

church. It will encourage you to find a home church quickly, and become loyal to the friends and leadership in your church. You will learn about the importance of loving and serving one another in a local church. You may have had bad experiences in the past with churches, but it doesn't have to be that way. Jesus created the church to help us, uphold us, and be our earthly family until He returns. It is faulty because it's made up of fallen people like you and me. But it can also be the greatest blessing if we love and care for one another.

The Christian life is filled with joys, blessing and trials! There is no yellow brick road without tribulation, this side of heaven. We hope you don't expect a life of comfort and peace now that you've made a commitment to follow Christ. Jesus was very clear that there would be trials, but He also said He would be there to help us through them. He promised us the grace, the power and strength to overcome our trials. In fact, as we undergo tribulations, they now become tools of God to build our character, and strengthen our faith. Faith doesn't grow through the easy times. Only problems bring about the fruit of patience and perseverance.

While there will be trials and persecutions, we can take comfort that there are also countless blessings for Christians, both in this life and the one to come. Those blessings come about as we follow Him, learn to be His disciples and live according to His will in the Kingdom of God.

So whatever you do, read this book from cover to cover. It's only a small book, you can do it! Don't rush through it. Take the time to absorb the information that each chapter provides. Examine the scriptures listed at the end of each chapter. Look them up in your Bible and read the chapter of the Bible in which they are contained. Through this process you are "growing in the grace and knowledge of God." You are becoming a disciple of Jesus, which is exactly what He wants you to become.

It will not end with this book. Hopefully, your study will make you eager to learn more, to study the Bible for yourself, and discipleship. But start here. Because you need to start. So get going!

Introduction

When Jesus came before Pontius Pilate, Pilate wanted to know if He really was a king and what He hoped to accomplish. Jesus said, *"You say rightly that I am a king. For this reason I was born, and for this reason I have come into the world, that I should bear witness to the truth. Everyone who is of the truth hears My voice." (John 18:37)*

Pilate's somewhat sardonic response was, "What is truth?" And that question has been echoed down through the centuries almost as a rallying cry for those who don't want to be held to any absolute standard.

Since the beginning, people have tried to avoid truth and its consequences by deliberately denying its existence. They say, "What is true for you may not necessarily be true for me." That expression has a spiritual cousin which says that "There are many ways to God, and all are equally valid." Phrases like these come across as being tolerant and accepting of other people's beliefs, but because of that, they are dangerously deceptive.

Any serious examination of all the belief systems in this world would easily expose the fallacy that "all roads lead to God". Buddhism, Hinduism, Islam, New Age and all the other religions contradict each other in just about every major aspect of their doctrines. From a strictly logical perspective, they can't all be correct!

The bottom line is that the underlying motive for acceptance of diversity is selfishness. It relieves people of any personal responsibility for facing an absolute truth and having to respond to it. They can feel free to believe anything they want. That means they can create a morality that suits their personal lifestyles, without having to be accountable to a higher "truth". In other words they don't have to answer to the commandments of God.

In their quest for personal justification, they go even farther. They say that those people who do believe there is a God, a God who has given us absolute values of right and wrong, are intolerant, narrow-minded, and bigoted. And in their scramble to absolve themselves of any personal responsibility they have created moral and ethical standards out of their own personal biases. There is no foundation for what they believe, other than the fact that they want to believe it! And they want others to believe it, so that they can continue in their lifestyles without external judgments of any kind. So, to remind them of the existence of rules of law like the Ten Commandments is an affront, and perceived as criticism and meddling in their personal affairs.

The irony is that if people only stopped struggling with justifying themselves and began to pursue the real truth, their battle for personal freedom would be over! Jesus said "Come to Me, all you who labor and are heavy laden, and I will give you rest. Take My yoke upon you and learn from Me, for I am gentle and lowly in heart, and you will find rest for your souls." (Matthew 11:28-29)

The peace and fulfillment that people are looking for is founded on the truth of God and the salvation available through the Gospel of Jesus Christ. Jesus made it clear to all of us when He said "If you abide in My word, you are My disciples indeed. And you shall know the truth, and the truth shall make you free." (John 8:31-32)

This book is dedicated to that truth in all its purity and power. As you search these pages and do what it says to do, you will be walking in the promises of Jesus. And there is no place more free in the universe.

"Therefore if the Son makes you free, you shall be free indeed." (John 8:36)

~ CHAPTER ONE ~

The Adventure Begins!

This book is written for two groups of people. Both of these groups are equally important and both will receive the same blessing if they follow the instructions contained here. One group consists of those of you who have been Christians for some time, but want to get off on a better foot than when you first began. Sometimes, through no fault of their own, people get off track. They've never really received solid instruction and built a proper foundation for their faith. Their growth has been stunted. If you're like that, you may be a strong believer, with a good relationship with God, but you may struggle with issues and habit patterns that get in the way of receiving the "fullness of joy" which God desires for all His children. This book is an ideal way to get back to the beginning and do it right this time!

The other group are those who have recently given their hearts to Jesus for the first time. If you've just recently become a Christian, welcome to the family of God! We know that God is delighted that you've chosen to follow Him and make Jesus your Lord and Savior. The Bible says there is great joy in heaven when someone becomes a new

Christian, because it means another person has accepted the free gift of God and been given eternal life. You're in for an exciting time! Contrary to what some may tell you, living for Jesus is never boring, so hang on and enjoy the ride. The next obvious question is "Where do I go from here?" Well, in the long term, that will depend largely on what God's plan is for you, but for the short term, there are some things you can - and should do, to help you on your way as a new child of God.

I'll never forget the day I committed myself to follow Jesus and become what my non-Christian friends disdainfully called a "born again" Christian. It was at the end of many weeks of soul searching and exploration. When I began my research it was probably the last thing I expected to happen! But there I was, at 2 a.m. surrendering myself to God and receiving His free gift of eternal life.

I was a television journalist and prided myself on my objectivity. So when my wife, Sandy, began to attend church and express an interest in spiritual things, I was tolerant of her new interest. After all, I was a man of reason and generosity! If it made her happy, why not let her pursue them? Little did I know that she was praying for me! Events began to take place in my life which caused me to examine my personal belief system. As my personal career became rocky, I realized I needed more answers than my own philosophies could provide. I decided to bring my journalism skills to bear on the subject of Christianity. All of my research and reading brought me to a particular point on a particular day in the Summer of 1981 when I felt a rush of realization that Jesus was really the Son of God! I saw that He really had died for my sins, and that everything the Bible said was true. It left me breathless and exhilarated at the same time. I had no choice. Given what I knew, I was compelled to surrender my life to the Creator of the Universe. My wife joined me in that prayer, and I can only imagine how excited and pleased she must have been. After earnestly praying that I would become a Christian, she saw her prayers come to pass.

A few short months later, Sandy and I and our three children were on our way to a discipleship training school, to begin the amazing adventure that would be the rest of our lives. I had given up my job, sold our home (in a market where they said nothing was selling!), and responded to God's prompting. We were to become involved in spreading the gospel of the good news of eternal life through Jesus Christ. I was living the journalist's ultimate dream! Journalists are always looking for that perfect piece of news which they can tell the rest of the world with earthshaking results. I had found the greatest news story ever, and most of us were ignoring or ridiculing it. From that time to this, it has been my happy job to get the news out in any way I can.

But I found out there's a lot more to Christianity than the first flush of belief. That's only the beginning! If Christians are going to stay in the faith and grow strong, there are some basic things they have to know and practice. I found out that if people don't learn and do these basic things, it won't be long before their enthusiasm grows weak, and Satan comes in to steal their faith. These practices are vital to a strong, growing Christian life. If that's what you want, then this small book will get you on your way!

Action Point

Everyone has a story about how God got their attention and brought them to faith in Him, and the salvation Jesus offers. Take the time now to write down a brief description about your life before you became a Christian, and how your life has changed. What was it like then? Besides the consequences of eternity without God, what else has God rescued you from?

~ Chapter Two ~

What Has Happened?

First, let's take a look at what has just happened in your life, and what it means. When you became a Christian you entered a new kingdom, the "Kingdom of Light". The apostle Peter said, Jesus *"...has called you out of darkness into His marvelous light." (1 Peter 2:9)*

(Note: The numbers and names I'll sometimes write in brackets are to help you locate Bible verses. They give you the "address" of the verse which has just been mentioned. For example, that last verse was in the first book of Peter, Chapter Two, Verse 9. Look it up for yourself and you'll see the whole verse and the context it was written in.)

Repent, you sinner!

The first thing you do to become a believer is to repent. When Jesus began His ministry, he urged people to: "...repent, for the Kingdom of God is here!" (Matthew 4:17).

Repentance literally means a change of mind, leading to a change of direction in your life. It implies that you have:

- Confessed to God that you are a sinner, and that your past life has been one of running away from God and His commands. You're not telling God anything He doesn't know, but you need to acknowledge it for your own sake.

- The second part of repentance is that you now turn from your sin and resolve not to live that kind of life any longer. Instead of continuing to pursue sinful habits, you now decide to pursue the things of God.

This doesn't guarantee you will immediately stop sinning! We still have our sinful natures and we will still fall into sin from time to time. But when we repent we are saying that sin is no longer our life's intention. We are telling God we now choose to move away from that lifestyle towards a life of righteousness. We'll talk a little more about this later and how it really needs to be a part of our lifestyle.

The next step is to admit that **you cannot save yourself.** No one sinking into a pit of quicksand can pull himself out! He needs a helping hand. God provided that help in the person of Jesus Christ, who paid the price for your sins by dying on a cross. God then showed he had victory over death by *raising Jesus from the dead.* As a result Jesus is able to offer you salvation *as a free gift.* All you have to do is accept the gift of salvation by recognizing that:

- Jesus is the Messiah, the Son of God.

- That He died for your sins.

- That your sins are forgiven because He paid the penalty.

The result of this is the most momentous news in cosmic history! (that's the journalist in me coming out.) **It's called the gospel of Jesus Christ.** And when you believe in the gospel, here is what happens:

1. **Your sins are washed away.** Revelation 1:5 describe Jesus as the one, "..who loved us and washed us from our sins in His own blood."

2. You become an adopted child of God with all the benefits that entails. John 1:12 says that "to those who received Him he gave the right to become the children of God." And according to Acts 26:18 Jesus says that entitles each of us to "...receive forgiveness of sins and an inheritance among those who are sanctified by faith in Me (Jesus)". This means we are citizens of a new Kingdom, with an eternal inheritance!

3. The third thing that happens is that **you become a new creation.** The apostle Paul says that now you have received Jesus into your lives, you are a "...new creation. Old things are passed away. Behold all things have become new." (2 Corinthians 5:17) This means we have been reborn in Christ. Our spirits have come alive. Our old lives are in the past. We can start afresh. We have a new hope, a new future and a new life that no one can take away from us!

I told you it was good news.

Because of His Love...

I've just told you of three of the promises and provisions that God has given to those who believe. But the best news is the answer to the question, "why". Why would God want to give us eternal life? The simple answer is that He wants to have a loving relationship with us.

Salvation is not based on some legal requirement which Jesus fulfilled on our behalf (which He did, and which is wonderful all by itself). But salvation exists because God loves us, and He did what He did because He wants to build a loving, mutual relationship with us that will last for eternity! John 3:16 says that *"God so loved the world (that's us!) that He gave His only Son, that whoever believed in Him would not perish, but instead have everlasting life."*

If we fail to see the motivation behind what God does, we will forever miss an awesome insight into His heart. The devil wants us to see God in a very different way than he actually is, and so we sometimes have the impression that God is a disapproving authority figure, waiting to slap us down the first time we do something wrong. But we were never created by God to be slapped down! As the Bible says, we were created *"in His image and likeness."* From the beginning, His desire has been to have fellowship with us. To bring us back to that relationship with Him, the Bible talks about us being transformed into His image, *"from glory to glory"(2 Corinthians 3:18).* <u>God wants to bring us into His Kingdom, and He's not going to let the fall of Adam stand in His way!</u>

God is sovereign. He will find ways to draw us to Him. So you can be sure that He's been speaking to your heart, even when you weren't consciously aware of it. If you are honest, you'll look back over your life and realize there's been a longing for God's Spirit in you for some time. Jesus said that, *"...No one can come to Me unless the Father who sent Me draws him." (John 6:43).* God is always the initiator of the relationship. There wouldn't even be a way to salvation and relationship with God unless God had initiated it in the first place. *"...God demonstrates His own love toward us, in that while we were still sinners, Christ died for us." (Romans 5:8).*

This places us in a very unique position in relationship to the Lord. Even though we didn't have the ability to understand what was going on; even though we were in a place of total rebellion against Him, God has arranged to fulfill his plan through Jesus. How great is His power, His glory, and His love for us!

Jesus did what He did, not only out of duty, but out of love and compassion. He came to *"set the captives free, heal the broken hearted, and give sight to the blind." (Luke 4:18).* The heart of God is for us to be free of our hangups and bad habits. Believing that Jesus died on the cross for your sins isn't simply a ticket to heaven, great as that is. It's the beginning of a lifetime of growing in love and understanding between you and God. As the song says, "We've only just begun!"

The Main Points Again...

As a new Christian you must:

1. Confess you have been a sinner, running from God.

2. Repent from your lifestyle and ask God's forgiveness.

3. Receive the free gift of salvation by believing that Jesus is the Divine Son of God, and that He died for your sins.

4. **Thank God for His forgiveness and the gift of eternal life.**

You are now a born again Christian and an adopted child of God. You are a "new creation" with a new eternal destiny and a new future.
All these things are given to you by God because He loves you and wants to build a relationship with you.

Action Point

Make sure you have processed the four points mentioned above. Not everyone goes through those points step by step, and in that order. Our relationship with God and his offer of salvation is too personal and individual to reduce to a formula, but in some way salvation means you have done what those four points talk about. Read them carefully and make sure in you're heart, that you've done what each point talks about.

Scriptures to Read and Memorize.

(Select at least one scripture to memorize right away. But make an effort to memorize them all. You will find them valuable to know in the future!)

But you are a chosen generation, a royal priesthood, a holy nation, His own special people, that you may proclaim the praises of Him who called you out of darkness into His marvelous light; (1 Peter 2:9)

But as many as received Him, to them He gave the right to become children of God, to those who believe in His name. (John 1:12)

For by grace you have been saved through faith, and that not of yourselves; it is the gift of God, not of works, lest anyone should boast. (Ephesians 2:8-9)

Therefore, if anyone is in Christ, he is a new creation; old things have passed away; behold, all things have become new. (2 Corinthians 5:17)

For God so loved the world that He gave His only begotten Son, that whoever believes in Him should not perish but have everlasting life. (John 3:16)

The Spirit of the LORD is upon me, because He has anointed me to preach the gospel to the poor; He has sent me to heal the brokenhearted, to proclaim liberty to the captives and recovery of sight to the blind, to set at liberty those who are oppressed; (Luke 4:18)

~ Chapter Three ~

What Can I Expect?

As you begin your new life in Christ, you will experience many thoughts and emotions. We all respond differently, and with different degrees of intensity, but you may probably feel one or more of these:

You feel more alive! Don't be surprised if colors seem more brilliant and there's a new spring in your step. In many ways it's like falling in love, except that you're in love with the Creator of the Universe!-And the wonder of it is that He loves you. This new awareness is bound to make everything seem fresh, because *you really are born again,* and you have a new purpose in life. That definitely happened to me. Every morning I woke up with an increasing excitement. I couldn't wait to get out of bed because this was a new day and I was going to learn more about Him! It's a great-to-be-alive kind of feeling.

Inner peace. This comes from making your peace with God. It's the feeling of "coming home". Jesus said *"Peace I leave with you, My peace I give to you. Not as the world gives..." (John 14:27)* This is the kind of peace the world cannot understand because it comes from the only true Divine source. The peace of Christ is able to overcome all anxiety, as we submit ourselves to Him. When I became a Christian, nothing could shake me! It seemed like I knew that everything was going to work out regardless of what the external circumstances were. Yes, real life does impact on us, and tragic things do happen from time to time, but that peace from God is still there, and it gives us a heavenly perspective!

You may begin to feel "conviction". Conviction means a recognition of sinful thoughts, attitudes or actions in your life. It shows itself in a sense of discomfort or even a very vivid realization when you do something wrong.

I'll never forget the first time the Holy Spirit spoke to me. I had a problem with swearing (among many other things) and one day I was by myself practicing my pool shot in the recreation room at work. I missed the shot and the first words out of my mouth were "Jesus Christ". And I wasn't praying! At that moment I felt a pain go through my heart like a hot poker. I knew that God was very directly telling me that my language was not appropriate and would have to change! It was going to be a long road to become the man God wanted me to be.

What I felt was the conviction of the Holy Spirit. I knew that from then on, my life was never going to be the same. The difference was, He was in me! And He wasn't about to let me get away with the same old stuff.

So if you feel those same convictions, rejoice! It's the Holy Spirit nudging your conscience, and from now on, you can't easily behave the way you used to! You're not as free to lie or swear or gossip, or do anything you know is not pleasing to God. God is at work in you, *"...and He who began a good work in you will complete it.." (Philippians 1:6)*

The Bible suddenly makes a whole lot of sense! If you used to read the Bible before you became a Christian, it may have seemed unclear or boring, or both! Maybe you thought it was just a bunch of foolish platitudes. But now there's new clarity. Phrases leap up from the page at you! The Bible seems to be talking directly to you. This is the Holy Spirit bringing God's word to life.

Jesus told us this would happen! He said in John 14:26 that, *"...the Helper, the Holy Spirit whom the Father will send in my name, He will teach you all things. And he will bring to your remembrance all the things that I have said to you."* The Apostle Paul said: *"Now we have not received the spirit of the world, but the Spirit who is from God, that we might know the things that have been freely given us by God."* (1 Corinthians 2:12)

Confusion and doubt. Be aware of the tactics of the devil! There's a lot to learn, a lot that seems strange to you, and the habits of a lifetime die hard. Old friends may call you crazy, and Satan surely doesn't want you in God's Kingdom! So questions and doubts are sure to come up. The devil will try to convince you it was just the emotion of the moment. You might even doubt whether God has really forgiven you, or whether you're really even saved. Don't be alarmed. Just because you have doubts doesn't mean you've lost your salvation.

If we had to do something to earn it, we might be justified in thinking that we could lose it somehow, but remember: salvation is a gift! There is not one of us on this planet who deserves salvation. None of us can earn our way. God did it because He loves us! Jesus died for us, says the Bible, *"while we were still sinners..."* (Romans 5:8)

Paul tells us, *"...it is by grace you have been saved through faith, and this not from yourselves, it is the gift of God, not by works, so that no-one can boast."* (Ephesians 2:8,9)

Our assurance is not from anything we can do, or whether we feel saved, **it's because of what Jesus did.** All we have to do is *receive it by faith.* Even our faith is a gift from God!

The Main Points Again...

Fill in the blanks.
When you become a Christian, you can expect one or more of the following experiences:

You feel more _____! Is this true in your life?

Inner _____. Why would you feel that?

You may begin to feel _____. What is it and where does it come from?

The Bible suddenly makes a whole lot of _____. Is this happening to you? What areas is God teaching you about?

Confusion and _____. Have you felt under attack lately? Are you beginning to question your experience? What are you supposed to do about it?

Action Point

Write down the experiences you first felt when you first believed. Did any of your emotions match the ones described in this chapter? Explain how they were similar or different. Don't forget, your salvation is based on faith in God, not emotion, so don't worry if your experiences don't match!

Scriptures to Read and Memorize.

Peace I leave with you, My peace I give to you; not as the world gives do I give to you. Let not your heart be troubled, neither let it be afraid. (John 14:27)

...being confident of this very thing, that He who has begun a good work in you will complete it until the day of Jesus Christ; (Philippians 1:6)

But the Helper, the Holy Spirit, whom the Father will send in My name, He will teach you all things, and bring to your remembrance all things that I said to you. (John 14:26) "

But God demonstrates His own love toward us, in that while we were still sinners, Christ died for us. (Romans 5:8)

Therefore submit to God. Resist the devil and he will flee from you. (James 4:7)

~ Chapter Four ~

Believe it by Faith

That brings us to the gift of faith. The Bible says that Jesus is "the author and finisher of our faith." (Hebrews 12:2). It defines faith as: "... being sure of the things we hope for and certain of the things we do not see." (Hebrews 11:1). Faith doesn't rest on feelings. We don't seek a sign or a light in the sky confirming what we've been told. *We simply believe.* It is that act of faith which justifies us. The Bible said that "Abraham believed and it was counted as righteousness". We are asked to believe in Jesus and in the Father who raised Jesus from the dead, and we are counted as righteous. That "righteousness" comes from the only One who never sinned. When we believe in Him, we are cloaked in His righteousness and that gives us the blessing of eternal life! As Paul said in his letter to the Romans:

> *"Therefore, having been justified by faith, we have peace with God through Jesus Christ, through whom we have gained access by faith into this grace in which we now stand. And we rejoice (exult) in the hope of the glory of God." (Romans 5:1-2)*

Stand Fast!

The Bible says: *"Stand fast in the faith. Be brave. Be strong."* There are plenty of answers which God provides in the Bible, but there will inevitably come questions which don't seem to have an answer. That's okay. If you knew all the answers you wouldn't need faith! In fact, when you don't have the answers, the answer *is* faith. Many people have spent a lot of time agonizing over parts of the Bible they didn't understand, or struggling with questions of life and theology that they couldn't reconcile with their understanding of God. Of course we will never truly understand God! Even when we're in heaven, in His mighty presence, He will be beyond our total understanding, because He's infinite and we're not. However, all of our questions will be answered with crystal clarity when we get to heaven and see God "face to face". But for now we "see in a mirror dimly'" as it says in 1 Corinthians 13:12.

In man's natural understanding, it can be very frustrating to have to make a decision to believe in God with unanswered questions. But remember this: before you become a Christian, you do not have all your faculties about you. One critical area is missing. Your spirit is dead! It only comes alive after you take that step of faith. Then you will receive new understanding, because you will be able to receive by the Spirit of God! Paul talks about that in 1 Corinthians 2.

" no one knows the things of God. Now we have received, not the spirit of the world, but the Spirit who is from God, that we might know the things which have been freely given to us by God... but the natural man does not receive the things of the Spirit of God, for they are foolishness to him; nor can he know them for they are Spiritually discerned." (1 Corinthians 2:12, 14)

That's why we are asked by God to be people of faith. Because only by faith will we be able to understand the things of the Spirit! Some people say, "if only I understand more, then I will believe." But God says, "If only you will believe, then all your questions will be answered!"

There comes a time when you simply must trust God. Have faith in His love and character. This will please Him. *"Without faith it is impossible to please God." (Hebrews 11:6)*

You will find that God wants to encourage you to grow in faith. He wants to show Himself to you in many different ways, *so that you will know He is there and actively involved in your life.* Many Christians are weak in their faith because they haven't given God the opportunity to be real in their lives. Instead, they've chosen to walk the safe road and make sure that whatever they do, it happens within the realm of their own limited capabilities. But God wants you to go beyond your own capabilities! He wants you to step out in faith because then He can reveal Himself, and strengthen your faith in the process.

Let me give you an example. When we sold our belongings and became involved in full-time missions, we realized we were going to have to trust God for our daily provision. That was taken care of almost immediately after we finished our training when the missions agency offered us a position as communications coordinator. We had a place to live and our meals were provided. Everything else we had to raise money for, but our needs were few because our children were young and we were just happy to be serving the Lord in this way. But then God really put us to the test! We were invited to a wedding in a town 400 miles away. Our daughter was to be the flower girl. But we had no money! How would we pay for the gas to get there and back?

As Sandy and I discussed the situation, we felt very clearly that this was going to be a test of our faith. God wanted us to believe that He would provide. So we prayed together that God would show us He wanted us to go. Deliberately, we told no-one that we needed money for gasoline. If God was going to come through, we wanted to be sure we knew it was Him! The next day, when we went to the mailbox, sure enough, there was an envelope with our name on it. When we opened it we saw that it contained enough cash to provide gas for the trip there, but not enough for the return! Our dilemma was obvious. In the town where we were going, we knew no one, except the bride. How would we get the cash to come home? Was this money a sign to go and trust God for the return, or were we being foolish in stepping out like that? Again, we prayed, and asked God to help us.

When we prayed, we clearly felt we were supposed to go and that God would somehow provide. We arrived at the town with our family and the family of the bride put us up in the home of some friends they knew; a delightful Russian family. They came from a conservative Christian background, spoke little, but were pleasant to be with. We stayed with them for a couple of days and enjoyed a wonderful traditional Russian wedding. Then God seemed to almost delight in showing us what He could do, if we let Him. We went through the reception line to greet the new bride and groom. We stopped and hugged the bride, offering our congratulations. She beamed at us and thanked us for coming, and then said, "Oh! I have something for you." She reached somewhere into the folds of her dress and pulled out an envelope. She gave it to Sandy and said, "This is to help pay for your gas to get here. We know you made a sacrifice to come." It was enough to get us home!

But wait! God wasn't finished yet. When we went to our host family to thank them for their hospitality, they also gave us an envelope. Inside was one hundred dollars! Sandy protested to them that we shouldn't take the money, but the man of the house raised up his hand and said, "It is not a question whether you should take the money. It is not from us; it is from God!" We stammered our thanks, and started home, overwhelmed at God's faithfulness. On our way back to the mission, we stopped at the small church where we had first given our lives to the Lord, and decided to go to the Wednesday evening service. They recognized us and decided to take an offering for us! We left that church with an additional thousand dollars! It was as if God was saying, "See, if you trust in Me, look at how much I will show Myself to you!" It was a sign to us that God was pleased with our steps of faith.

So we know that God is pleased when we step out in obedience in this way; it gives Him the opportunity to be God in our lives. It's not always about money, although God does seem to use finances a lot! We have seen God be faithful in countless other ways. You will too, if you simply realize that *God wants to show Himself faithful to you, and stretch your faith!*

It is through the process of stretching your faith that your faith grows. Makes sense when you look at it that way! But it's a truth that many Christians don't want to put into practice because it takes them beyond their comfort zones. They don't realize they're missing out on some of life's greatest blessings, to see God come through in answer to their faith!

One other point while we're on the subject of faith. Faith is not a "leap" into the unknown. Most non-Christians mock faith, because they believe it's the same as "fantasy". But proper faith is founded on reason and research. God said, "Come let us reason together." He doesn't want blind followers.

Faith is definitely a step out into the unknown, but it is based on God's Word, His promises, His character and historical events that have been recorded and confirmed over time. There's more actual written evidence to believe in the life, death and resurrection of Jesus than there is to believe in Julius Caesar!

The more you stretch your faith and see God work in your lives, the more personal evidence you will have of God's truth and faithfulness.

The Main Points Again...

• What is faith? (See Hebrews 11:1)

• If we have faith in God, how does God see us?

• If we have faith, does that mean we must never doubt?

• What is the best way for us to grow in our faith?

Action Point

This could become exciting! God wants you to begin stretching your faith right away. Ask him for specific answers to prayer so that you know He is answering. Also, ask him to give you a test of obedience, so that you can step out in faith and see God respond. Be ready to tell someone how God revealed Himself to you this week!

Scriptures to Read and Memorize.

Now faith is the substance of things hoped for, the evidence of things not seen. (Hebrews 11:1)

Therefore, having been justified by faith, we have peace with God through our Lord Jesus Christ, through whom also we have access by faith into this grace in which we stand, and rejoice in hope of the glory of God. (Romans 5:1-2)

Watch, stand fast in the faith, be brave, be strong. Let all that you do be done with love.
(1 Corinthians 16:13-14)

But without faith it is impossible to please Him, for he who comes to God must believe that He is, and that He is a rewarder of those who diligently seek Him.
(Hebrews 11:6)

~ Chapter Five ~

What Do I Do Now?

The Bible says that you are now a child of God, and *"seated in the heavenly places with Christ" (Ephesians 2:6)*. That means God sees us as citizens of His kingdom, and because of the saving work of Jesus, God identifies us as being in God's Kingdom with Him. Welcome to your new citizenship! However, you may have noticed your body still has to live here in this world! You may also have noticed that, while you're now a Christian, your bad habits and attitudes didn't just go away. You're just more painfully aware of them! Well God accepts us just as we are, but He doesn't want us to stay that way. He wants to clean us up. We want to help you to develop good Christian habits and give you the tools you need to change your lifestyle. You will find that, as you draw closer to God, *He will do the changing in you, from the inside out.*

You will also be asked to play a part in your growth. The word "discipline" comes from the same root as the word "disciple". So, it shouldn't come as a surprise that being a disciple of Jesus will require effort. You're dealing with the habits of a lifetime. God can and does miraculously take away past habits, but more often He works with us as we deal with the consequences of life. Soon we find we have victory over those sinful habits, because the Holy Spirit has helped us to overcome them! He is changing us to become *"...conformed to the image of His Son." (Romans 8:29)* - and that is worth more than anything else in the world.

The first thing you need to do as a Christian is get a proper understanding of your place in the universe, and your relationship to God. God gave us the key to this relationship in the Old Testament, and Jesus emphasized it again when he spoke to one of the scribes, a religious leader in the community. The scribe said, "Teacher which is the greatest law of all?" Jesus said:

"You shall love the LORD your God with all your heart, with all your soul, and with all your mind. This is the first and great commandment. And the second is like it: You shall love your neighbor as yourself."(Matthew 22:37)

You may have heard this before, but it's time to look at it again with new eyes! In our upside down world we've got it all wrong. The key to getting a real sense of peace and fulfillment is to stop putting ourselves first!

We live in a me-first society and people are miserable because they're wrapped up in themselves. But when we finally realize that there is a Creator of the Universe and He is all powerful, all-knowing and all-loving, it makes no sense to concentrate on "poor little me!" God says the secret is stop worrying about yourself, and PUT GOD FIRST! He is where all the answers lie. We know very little about life, and compared to God, what we do know is insignificant!

Peter told Jesus, *"You alone have the keys to eternal life."* And he was right! There's a constant longing in all of us to find the "meaning of life". God planted that desire there. As the Bible says, He has put "eternity in our hearts". Why? So we would search Him out and He would reveal to us the mysteries of the universe. As we put Him first, we find the satisfaction we've always been looking for.

There are people who look at Christianity and say, "That seems like a good idea. But I don't want to give up all my other activities, so I'll just add God to the list of things in my life." I'm afraid that kind of thinking doesn't work with God. He's not too pleased to be treated like just another commodity. Just imagine if you said to your girl or boy friend, "I want to marry you, but I want to keep all these other lovers in my life too. You don't mind, do you!?"

God knows that if you try to live both sides of the fence, you will be forever miserable, because you will live a life of constant compromise. You will never overcome the world, and never truly belong to God. Sitting on a fence is a very uncomfortable position.

Jesus said you cannot serve two masters. Those that do will love one and hate the other. Trying to serve two masters is exactly where many Christians fail and stumble in their walk with God. You can't do it your way and God's way at the same time! That's why the Bible says: *"Trust in the Lord with all your heart and do not lean on your own understanding. In all your ways acknowledge him and He shall direct your paths."* *(Proverbs 3:5,6)*

Purify your heart

As you begin your Christian life, you already know that God has forgiven your sins and you have a clean slate. But that doesn't take away the sinful habits and attitudes you might still be involved in. That's why one of the earlier conditions we spoke about was repentance. It's important for you to repent of your past sins and also to *stay away from these sins in the future!*

This requires a deliberate effort on your part to cleanse yourself from sinfulness. If you don't, you will continue to fall into past habit patterns. If you really want to love God with your whole heart, soul, mind and strength, then it's a good idea to apply yourself to this purifying process.

It's not hard. All you have to do is ask God to show you the areas of your life which are not pleasing to Him. If they aren't pleasing to Him, it's because He knows they will lead you on the path of pain and destruction. This destruction will affect you and everyone around you, especially those closest to you. If you ask Him, He will show you the habits, attitudes and behavior which need to be stopped.

You might be shocked to find out what they are! A girl who became a Christian asked the Lord to show her areas of sin in her life and immediately He told her to stop living and sleeping with her boy friend. She had been so used to the standards of the society around her, it hadn't occurred to her it was a sin. But any sexual activity outside marriage is sinful.

Jesus forgave the woman who was caught by the Pharisees as an adulteress, but he also told her to "go and sin no more." He didn't want her going back to that same lifestyle. To do that is to ignore the commandments of God and to insult the salvation he has offered.

Ask God to show you your areas of sinfulness. Are they laziness? Geed? Lust? Jealousy? Anger? Unforgiveness? Pornography? If you ask the Holy Spirit, He will tell you, so you can repent of those sinful choices in your life, receive forgiveness for them and then resolve to stay away from those sins in the future. If you have not resolved to change your life in these areas, then you have not truly repented. And God is not first on your list.

You might think it will be difficult to turn away from sinful habits. You're right, it will! These things are pleasurable to you. That's why you do them! Sinful acts do feel good for the moment. But God also knows they eventually lead to death. Sin destroys self respect, character, relationship with God, sometimes death of the physical body, and eventually death of the soul. That's why they must go.

The difficulty in stopping these habits is much like stopping any addictive habit. You must replace the old habit with a new one. This requires discipline, and a resolve to avoid sin.

But it also requires something else, because sin cannot be conquered with will power alone. It requires calling on the power of the Holy Spirit to help you to overcome your sin. Remember, you have the the Lord on your side now. Paul said *"I can do all things through Christ, who gives me strength." (Philippians 4:13)*. You cannot do it yourself, but by faith in God, and His saving grace, you can do anything!

The second most important commandment is to love your neighbor as yourself. In other words, stop thinking of yourself as the center of the universe. The apostle Paul puts it this way: *"let each esteem others better than himself"*. *(Philippians 2:3)*

In our world the word "love" has really lost its meaning because it has so many meanings! But the Bible specifically talks about sacrificial love. In this definition, to love others means to want the best for that person. It does not mean we have to have a "warm fuzzy feeling" about the person. It just means we have their interests at heart, and that we at least treat them as well as we'd like to be treated!

When we begin to care for the concerns of others and minister to their needs, we find out our own concerns become relatively unimportant. We develop a compassion for the lost of this world, and our hearts are touched by the things which touch God's heart.

In the meantime, God continues to work in our lives through our concern for others. Caring requires that we be humble, not so concerned for our own well being or our own status in life. The Bible says that God is opposed to the proud, but gives grace to the humble. So being humble brings us favor with God - a very good place to be!

The Main Points Again...

What is the secret to discovering your place in the Universe?

Is God able to accept it if we include Him as one of the important parts of our lives?

What is the second most important commandment?

What does it mean to "love your neighbor"?

When we care for others, what characteristic does that develop in our lives?

Action Point

If you haven't begun already, make a list of areas which the Holy Spirit could be pointing out to you about your present lifestyles. Resolve to change your habits and ask God to help you develop a pure heart. The closer we get to the heart of God, the more we want to purify ourselves. Be sensitive to what your heavenly Father is showing you.

Scriptures to read and memorize.

But God, who is rich in mercy, because of His great love with which He loved us, even when we were dead in trespasses, made us alive together with Christ (by grace you have been saved), and raised us up together, and made us sit together in the heavenly places in Christ Jesus, (Ephesians 2:4-6)

Jesus said to him, "You shall love the LORD your God with all your heart, with all your soul, and with all your mind." This is the first and great commandment. And the second is like it: "You shall love your neighbor as yourself." (Matthew 22:37-39)

He has made everything beautiful in its time. Also He has put eternity in their hearts, except that no one can find out the work that God does from beginning to end. (Ecclesiastes 3:11)

Trust in the LORD with all your heart, And lean not on your own understanding; In all your ways acknowledge Him, and He shall direct your paths. (Proverbs 3:5-6)

God resists the proud, But gives grace to the humble. (James 4:6)

This is my commandment that you love one another as I have loved you. (John 15:12)

Chapter Six

The Disciplines of a Believer

Read The Manual!

Many of us are proud that we can "make it work" without even reading the manual. From computers to fixing cars, people say, "I don't need that, I can do it myself!" But, that's never very wise even in the physical realm. You might wreck the thing you're trying to fix! But for Christians, not reading the manual is a guarantee you're heading down the road to trouble!

The Bible is your operations manual. It has the answers to survival on this planet. The Bible itself says: *"All scripture is inspired by God and profitable for doctrine, reproof, correction and for instruction in righteousness." (2 Timothy 3:16)* Not only is it your training manual, but it's also your source of inspiration and strength. This book is not just for advice; it's also the source of your energy!

We should remember that the Bible is the inspired Word of God. When you read it, read with faith that God will speak to you through it. God said this about His word:

> *"So shall My word be that goes forth from My mouth;*
> *It shall not return to Me void,*
> *But it shall accomplish what I please,*
> *And it shall prosper in the thing for which I sent it."*
> *(Isaiah 55:11)*

God gave us the Bible to reveal who He is and to guide our lives. We are foolish if we try to live without reading it every day! Look at what it can do to help us:

- The Bible encourages us and shows us how to live righteous lives.

- It enables us to defeat the forces of darkness who try to tempt us to sin.

- It tells us all we need to know about God. If we want to know Him better, we should read His Word to us.

- The Holy Spirit speaks to us through scripture. He quickens verses to our minds and thoughts, so we know He is prompting us in certain ways. But He can only do this if we are reading the Bible regularly!

It's very important to develop a habit of reading the Bible or we will forget. Habits take time to develop, especially good habits! Try to find a special place and time you can call your own. This will help you to focus on what God is saying. And it will be a habit pattern that encourages you to read daily. Begin by reading the gospel of John and passages from the Psalms and the Epistles. There are many other ways to read the Bible and many plans available to help you to read regularly. It doesn't matter as long as you get into the habit!

Have a regular time of prayer.

Some people call this their quiet time or devotional time. It doesn't matter what you call it as long as you do it! You can combine your Bible reading with your prayer time, but they are two distinct activities. When you read your Bible, you are receiving spiritual insights and information from the Word of God. In prayer, you are in communication with your God. You talk to Him, He talks to you.

Prayer times are extremely important! They establish your relationship with God. You cannot get to know anyone without spending time with them. It's the same with God. You are on a journey to get to know Him. The best way to do that is through regular and consistent prayer. God gives us enough grace to live every day, but not enough for the following day. We need to make an appointment with Him daily. I've noticed in my own times with God, that if I skip a day, I miss it. Not only that, but I feel less able to cope with the stresses of every-day life. And if I miss more than a day, God will graciously get me through, but I can feel my spiritual tank getting emptier and emptier!

In the Bible it talks about how the people of Israel received manna from heaven every day while they were out in the wilderness. There was no food for them there, so God provided. It was a daily miracle! And it reminded them of God's love and provision every day. But God only provided them with enough for that day's needs. (Except for the Sabbath, when they were not allowed to go and pick the manna on that day. On Friday, God provided enough for two days!) We too, need to meet with God daily. We cannot depend upon yesterday's blessings, yesterday's grace, or yesterday's prayers to get us through today! God doesn't want us coming to Him on Sundays only!

How do you pray?

Remember that prayer is simply conversation with God. Of course, it goes deeper than that, too, until we achieve that place where we are truly in communion with Him. In fact, prayer is a place of truly supernatural blessing, where we can be in contact with His heart for us and for the whole world. These things come with time and experience. But for now, we can be satisfied to recognize that we can come to Him boldly and personally to share our deepest thoughts. He wants to meet with you too. So relax and come into His presence.

In your first times of prayer, you'll be getting to know each other. So you can speak to Him about your day, about your problems and fears. He isn't bored or indifferent. The things that concern you concern Him also. Nothing is too small, or too big to bring to God in prayer!

When you pray, it's always good to begin with thanksgiving. The Bible says *"Come into His presence with thanksgiving."* *(Psalm 95:2)* When we do that, we realize we have much to be grateful for! And that puts us in the right attitude. Giving praise to God always keeps us humble and thankful. Then we are ready to receive from Him, not grumbling or complaining about our lot in life.

Having said that, there are many times when things are going on in our life that we don't understand. We might even feel like complaining to God that life is just unfair! It's okay to tell God that; He can take it. He knows when we're having a problem anyway. We can't fool Him, so we might as well let Him know how we feel. But even then, it's a good idea to keep an "attitude of gratitude" for the many blessings He has given us. That helps us keep things in the right perspective. It's interesting that, if we come to God, first thanking Him for the many blessings in our lives, suddenly those things which were bothering us before don't seem to be quite so imposing or difficult to handle.

Prayer also means we take the time to listen! God wants to speak to us, but sometimes we're too busy. We rhyme off a whole list of things we want and need, then we hang up the phone before we get to hear what He has to say!

Before you finish that prayer, just for a minute, stop talking. Listen. Don't listen for audible voices! Listen to the promptings in your mind. God doesn't usually speak with a roar; He drops an idea or a thought in quietly. There's nothing mystical about hearing God. He speaks in the natural processes of our thoughts. You will be surprised at the way God will answer your prayers.

Pray for Others.

When you pray, pray for others first. Pray for your church, pastor, community, country. Pray for ministries you know about, pray for yourself and your family's needs. There will be times when He will ask you to pray in "spiritual warfare" (we'll explain that later), or to intercede on behalf of other people or countries. It's always a privilege to stretch our faith and pray for issues and concerns outside our own narrow world. If God asks you to pray for these kinds of issues, don't be afraid to do it. The faith you have as a new believer is more powerful than you think! New Christians can sometimes get their prayers answered faster and easier than older Christians, because their faith is fresher, and their enthusiasm is greater. Remember, whatever you think about, or worry about, or wonder about, is also worth praying about!

Pray believing He will answer! Remember, He wants to hear from you and He wants to answer the prayers of his children. The Bible says a lot about God's desire to answer prayer. In Mark, Jesus said *"whatever things you ask when you pray, believe that you receive them and you will have them." (Mark 11:24)*

Keep a Journal.

One of the best ways to keep track of your growth in the Lord and to see how God has been speaking to you, is to keep a journal. Some people have a daily time of "Bible meditation" where they read a passage of scripture, and ask God to reveal Himself to them through the scripture. Then, as they write, they sense God's promptings to help them in their daily lives. There are any number of ways to write your journal. There is no right or wrong way, just what makes you the most comfortable.

1. You can write your thoughts or, special scriptures as you read the Bible. This helps to clarify what you've read, and maybe bring into a clearer definition some thing the Holy Spirit is saying to you.

2. You can "talk to God" in your journal, explaining your feelings, or telling Him what you think He's trying to teach you, or simply to thank Him for what you're learning every day.

3. You can write to yourself, as God drops words of wisdom and truth into your mind, and you simply write them on paper. Of course, many times you might simply be writing your own imaginations, but as you look back over those pages, you will be surprised to see the insights you wrote without even knowing it.

A final thought about prayer. The more you do it, the easier it gets. None of these spiritual practices come naturally to us. That's because we aren't used to communicating in the spiritual realm! We are too easily distracted by the physical demands of our day, and the fact that we are uncomfortable, and we have to scratch, or go feed the dog, or pick up the laundry. Anything, but get down to pray! Sometimes we may be tempted to say, "It's too much work, and I don't know if it's accomplishing anything!" (see the chapter on faith!)

Prayer is the most fundamental thing we do to communicate with God. *But it does require an effort on our part.* Soon, as you enter into the place and regular practice of prayer, you will sense your body responding to the discipline you are putting it through. It will "settle down" and enter into a place of repose before God. Your heart will begin to link with the heart of your heavenly Father. You will enter into a place of peace, where you will be free to share your thoughts and listen to His gentle voice. It takes time, and diligence for that to happen. Don't give up! Your daily time with God can and should be the most rewarding part of your Christian life.

The Main Points Again...

Why should we read the Bible?

- The Bible _____ us, and shows us how to live righteous lives!

- It enables us to _____ the forces of darkness who try to tempt us to sin.

- If we want to _____.

- The Holy Spirit _____ through scripture.

Why is prayer important?

- They establish your _____ with God.

- We need to make an appointment with Him _____.

What is prayer?

- Prayer is simply _____ with God.

Who should you pray for? (Make your own personal list!)

What is a key factor in prayer?

- Pray _____ He will answer!

What are the advantages of keeping a journal?

1.

2.

3.

What is the Key to a productive time of prayer with your Father?

Action Point

Begin to put into practice the disciplines of this chapter. Set up a schedule for your time of prayer and Bible reading. Do not fail to do this; it's the most important habit you will ever develop!

Scriptures to Read and Memorize

All Scripture is given by inspiration of God, and is profitable for doctrine, for reproof, for correction, for instruction in righteousness (2 Timothy 3:16),

Let us come before His presence with thanksgiving; Let us shout joyfully to Him with psalms. (Psalms 95:2)

Therefore I exhort first of all that supplications, prayers, intercessions, and giving of thanks be made for all men, for kings and all who are in authority, that we may lead a quiet and peaceable life in all godliness and reverence. For this is good and acceptable in the sight of God our Savior, who desires all men to be saved and to come to the knowledge of the truth. (1 Timothy 2:1-4)

Therefore I say to you, whatever things you ask when you pray, believe that you receive them, and you will have them. (Mark 11:24)

One thing I have desired of the Lord, that will I seek after, that I may dwell in the house of the Lord all the days of my life to behold the beauty of the Lord and to enquire in His temple. (Psalm 27:4)

~ Chapter Seven ~

Believer's Baptism

As you pray and seek to be obedient to God, one of the things His word will quickly urge you to do, is to be baptized. When Peter preached to the multitudes on the day of Pentecost, and the crowds asked what they should do, Peter said *"Repent and be baptized in the name of Jesus Christ for the remission of sins. And you will receive the Holy Spirit." (Acts 2:38)* This is a clear command from God to show the world an outward sign of your inward commitment to Him.

It's clear that Jesus meant baptism to be a vital part of the beginning of a believer's life. He even told the disciples to go into the whole world and make disciples, *"baptizing them in the name of the Father and Son and Holy Spirit." (Matthew 28:19)*.

Baptism in water is the public declaration that you have given your life to Christ and intend to follow Him. In many countries where Christianity is persecuted, public baptism is a very dangerous thing to do, because everyone knows you are turning from your old religions and lifestyles to follow Jesus.

We lived for a while in a Middle Eastern country. (We won't mention the specific country for security reasons.) The religion in the Middle East is predominantly Muslim. It is forbidden by many Muslim countries to convert to any other religion, but especially to Christianity. The penalty for conversion is very serious, and can range from imprisonment to death. But even if the government did not put a new convert in jail and torture him or her, the Muslim family of the new Christian would be terribly upset. To convert to Christianity is like becoming a traitor. In the eyes of Muslims, Christianity is the enemy. Christians are infidels, heading for hell. In addition, the new convert has just covered the whole family with disgrace. The honor of the family has been tainted, and the only solution is to kill the one who is the cause. So, Muslims who convert to Christianity are in immediate danger for their lives!

It becomes even more serious when these converts become baptized. Some have even been baptized in bathtubs, with only a few members of the church present, so that their family doesn't find out. Others have boldly said they don't care what their family does, and have been baptized publicly. In some cases that has led to their arrest or their death. At the very least, these people lose their jobs and status in the community.

When new converts are baptized, they are declaring they have repented from their sinful past and are now living a new life, following Jesus, and joining in the membership of the church. The Bible says that *"by one Spirit, we were all baptized into one body." (1 Corinthians 12:13)* That body is the Church of Jesus Christ.

The Spiritual Importance of Baptism

Buried with Christ

There is also very definite spiritual significance to being baptized. Colossians 2:12 says, *"...you were...buried with Christ in baptism, in which you also were raised with Him through faith in the working of God, who raised Him from the dead."*

When we are baptized we are identifying with Christ's death and resurrection. That means that we, and all our sins, are "buried with Him." From the moment of our faith in Jesus, we have died to ourselves, and have been raised a new creation. Baptism symbolizes that our sins have been "washed away", so to speak, and our past is not to be held against us.

Newness of Life

Not only is the past forgiven, but we are empowered to live "a new life" by the power of God. The apostle Paul explains that in *Romans 6:4: "Therefore we were buried with Him through baptism into death, that just as Christ was raised from the dead by the glory of the Father, even so we also should walk in newness of life."* (emphasis mine.)

That empowering life takes place because Jesus has come to live in us, making us temples of God. We contain within our mortal bodies all that is needed to live the way God had intended. Not by our power! Not by our strength! We've already proven that doesn't work. But by the power of God, working in us. The Bible says, *"I have been crucified with Christ; it is no longer I who live, but Christ lives in me; and the life which I now live in the flesh I live by faith in the Son of God, who loved me and gave Himself for me."* (Galatians 2:20)

What an amazing and life-changing truth! We live, but now Christ is in us! And as we walk by faith in Him and what He did, Christ lives through us. *In these few words lies the secret of living a victorious Christian life.* We don't do it, Jesus does! Our job is to set our own desires and personal aspirations aside and allow Jesus to live through us.

In baptism, we are expressing the fact that our lives are buried with Him, and now we walk in a new life. It truly is a rebirth and a chance to start again with Christ. As God raised Jesus, so too are we raised up and are no longer slaves to sin. Through the power of the Holy Spirit we are equipped to break the bondage of sin in our lives.

Why be baptized by immersion?

I suppose we could become dogmatic and say because Jesus was baptized that way. It says in Matthew 6:13 that, *"...When He had been baptized, Jesus came up immediately from the water."* Jesus didn't always do everything a particular way just so we could copy him. However, there is a principle involved here, that baptism represents a death and resurrection. The only way to do that is to require immersion, unless there are extreme circumstances.

Baptism in the early church was by immersion. One example of this kind of baptism is in Acts 8:38, when Philip baptized an Ethiopian eunuch:

"And both Philip and the eunuch went down into the water, and he baptized him. Now when they came up out of the water, the Spirit of the Lord caught Philip away, so that the eunuch saw him no more; and he went on his way rejoicing."

A third reason to baptize by immersion is because that's what the word "baptism" means: to dip under water.

And finally, there's the witness of earlier church leaders. Martin Luther, John Calvin, and John Wesley all agreed that baptism should be by full immersion into the water.

When should I be baptized?

As soon as you have believed! The Bible is clear that believers are baptized right away: *"Then those who gladly received his word were baptized; and that day about three thousand souls were added to them."* Acts 2:41.

I've heard people say that they weren't ready to be baptized yet, because they weren't "good enough". Believe me, you'll never be good enough! That's the whole point: it's Jesus who washes you. It's His blood that was shed for your sins. It's His work, not yours that removes the sin. Of course you're not good enough! That's why He had to come and die for your sins, because only He is good enough.

Your job is not to become "good enough". It's to be obedient to His command to be baptized. He'll take care of the rest.

The Main Points Again...

• When we are baptized, what are we identifying with?

• What does that mean for us?

• Why should we be baptized?

Action Point

Be obedient! Be baptized!

Scriptures to Read and Memorize

Or do you not know that as many of us as were baptized into Christ Jesus were baptized into His death? Therefore we were buried with Him through baptism into death, that just as Christ was raised from the dead by the glory of the Father, even so we also should walk in newness of life. (Romans 6:3-4)

In Him you were also circumcised with the circumcision made without hands, by putting off the body of the sins of the flesh, by the circumcision of Christ, buried with Him in baptism, in which you also were raised with Him through faith in the working of God, who raised Him from the dead. (Colossians 2:11-12

Then those who gladly received his word were baptized; and that day about three thousand souls were added to them. (Acts 2:41)

~ Chapter Eight ~

Find a Good Bible-believing Church

A vital step to your Christian growth is fellowship with other believers. Trying to live a Christian life in this world without the help and friendship and prayers of other Christians is like walking out into a minefield blindfolded. Satan would just love you to try and make it on your own. There are no Christian Rambos! The enemy would tear them to shreds.

Let's face it; you're just getting started as a Christian. You need training, and nurturing. You need to know what spiritual weapons you have at your disposal and how to use them. You need to have people around who've been through what you're going through, and can encourage you and point you along the right roads. It would be foolish not to benefit from the wisdom of those who've gone before you. Many do try to go it alone, but it's because they get caught up in pride and independence. As Christians, we are all members of God's family, and God made us to depend on one another. Jesus said others would know we are Christians by the love we have for one another-not by our tough, macho image!

There are many churches with many different styles of worship. You can go from formal to informal, modern to traditional, charismatic to conservative, denominational to non-denominational. Some churches sing hymns which they've sung for many years. Others prefer newer songs with more contemporary styles of singing. There's nothing wrong with looking around to find a church which seems to suit you. But there are some basic doctrines that should always be there. The most important thing is that they worship God and teach the good news of salvation through Jesus. Here are some key things to look for:

- Find a church that believes the Bible is the inspired, inerrant Word of God. Inerrant simply means that God did not allow factual errors in the Bible. He may have allowed the writer's style and the culture of the era to come through, but He would not allow errors of fact or doctrine. A church which says the Bible can be wrong or faulty in some areas is one to avoid.

- Make sure the Church believes that Jesus Christ is the Messiah, the Son of God, and that, as the Son of God, He is completely God and completely man. That He came to earth as part of an eternal plan, and died on the cross to redeem us from our sins. And on the third day, He rose from the dead, conquering death and sin.

- Make sure the church believes in the Trinity. The trinity simply means that there is One God, and three persons in God: Father, Son, and Holy Spirit. The Holy Spirit is the third person of the Trinity. The Holy Spirit lives in us today, teaching, comforting, convicting us of sin, guiding our lives, and enabling us through His gifts to live Holy and righteous lives.

- Make sure the church believes the only way to salvation is through the gift of eternal life offered to us by Jesus Christ.

There are literally thousands of churches which believe these basic doctrines. But there are also many churches which say they are Christian but which do not believe those doctrines. Be on guard against false doctrines! Among them are the following:

- That Jesus was a good teacher but not God.

- That there are many ways to heaven and Christianity is just one of them

- That Jesus' death on the cross was for everyone, regardless of whether they believe in Him or accept Him. Therefore, everyone is already saved.

- That there are other books equal to or which take precedence over the Bible. Among these, you will find the Book of Mormon and the Muslim holy book called the Qur'an.

- That you can get to heaven through the good works that you do. You cannot make it to heaven by good works or Jesus wouldn't have had to die for our sins! This makes a mockery of what Jesus did for us on the cross. Of course, good works are important, but we are saved by grace, not by works. (Ephesians 2:8,9)

- That you must do other things besides accept the salvation of Christ. The early Jews wanted all Christians to be circumcised. Paul warns us against putting legal additions to the gospel. He said, *"Beware, lest anyone cheat you through philosophy and empty deceit, according to the tradition of men, according to the basic principles of the world and not according to Christ." (Colossians 2:8)* He added, *"So let no-one judge you in food or in drink, or regarding a festival or a new moon or sabbaths." (2:16)*

- Some groups teach we can become gods, and that we are destined to become like God. That's the same lie that

Satan told Adam and Eve in the garden! It's a statement that appeals to our pride, and our desire to want to "do it ourselves". Be wary of those who would tell you those things. There's nothing wrong with trying to be better than you are, but we can't be like God. For one thing, we are created beings, and had a beginning! God never had a beginning; He is eternal.

• Speaking of Satan, some churches teach that Satan is not a living being, but only a "personification of evil." But the Bible teaches that Satan and his followers are real, although Satan would like us to think otherwise.

• And finally, some churches want to use only certain sections of the Bible and disregard those they disagree with. Therefore they say certain activities which the Bible calls sin are acceptable, or alternative lifestyles. Christians are accused of being judgmental when we point out what the Bible says about immoral living. But we are only pointing out God's eternal commandments. It's not up to us to pass judgment. But there will come a time when God will judge everyone. As Christians we should lovingly point out what the Bible says in the hope that people will recognize and want to repent of their sins.

In conclusion, stay away from churches which teach a partial or false gospel. Paul said many would crop up in the last days, and he was right.

The Main Points Again...

What are the key things to look for in a church?

• Find a church that believes the Bible is the inspired, _____ Word of God.

• Make sure the Church believes that Jesus Christ is the Messiah, the _____.

• Make sure the church believes in the _____.

• Make sure the church believes the only way to salvation is through the gift of _____ offered to us by _____.

What kind of churches should I avoid?

• That Jesus was a good teacher but not _____

• That there are many ways to heaven and _____ is just one of them.

• That Jesus' death on the cross was for everyone, regardless of whether they _____ Him.

• That there are other books _____ the Bible

• That you can get to heaven through the _____ that you do.

• That you must _____ besides accept the salvation of Christ

• Some groups teach we can _____.

- Some churches teach that Satan is not _____
_____.

- Some churches want to use only _____ of the
Bible and disregard those they _____.

Action Point

You may already be a member of a church, in which case
you simply need to continue by plugging yourself in and
become involved! But if you're not attending a church, start
looking for one immediately.

Scriptures to Read and Memorize

*Now, therefore, you are no longer strangers and for-
eigners, but fellow citizens with the saints and members of
the household of God, having been built on the foundation
of the apostles and prophets, Jesus Christ Himself being
the chief cornerstone, (Ephesians 2:19-20)*

*And I also say to you that you are Peter, and on this
rock I will build My church, and the gates of Hades shall
not prevail against it. (Matthew 16:18)*

*And He is the head of the body, the church, who is the
beginning, the firstborn from the dead, that in all things
He may have the preeminence.(Colossians 1:18)*

~ Chapter Nine ~

After You've Found Your Church...

Stay at the church you've chosen.

When you've chosen a good Bible-believing church, you should make a commitment to stay at that church. Of course, you should attend a few to find out what they are like, and to find one that suits you, but once you've found a church you like, **make a commitment to stay.** There will never be a perfect church because it's made of imperfect people, and that includes you! You will probably discover things or people that you don't like. That's life. Stick it out anyway, because it'll be the same wherever you go. Only when you put down roots are you able to allow God to help you grow and develop good Christian relationships. You should only consider leaving if you disagree seriously with what the church teahes, if you feel the leadership is too controlling, or if the church condones, or ignores serious sin.

Pray for your Church. When you have found a church home, you should support that church with your prayers. God tells us to pray for our spiritual leaders and give them respect. This is very important if you want your church to remain healthy.

Become involved. Join in the church Bible Studies, adult Sunday Schools or discipleship programs. These programs will encourage you to dig into God's word, meet with like-minded believers, and grow spiritually. It's good for you to like the pastor of your church. But keep in mind the pastor is not the only person you can learn from in your church! The Holy Spirit provides gifts to people within the church to help one another. There are people with the gift of teaching, and people who are able to pray with you and encourage you. And you will meet people in your small groups who will become your best and closest friends. These are the ones you will confide in and trust and pray with as you grow in your faith.

Give to your Church. It's a Biblical principle to give to the place where you are being spiritually fed. This is important for the health and growth of your church. Your church reaches out into the community, pays for staff and provides the buildings and ministries through your giving. The church is only as effective as the generosity of the people who attend.

Giving is also important for your own spiritual well being. Much of our identity is wrapped up in our finances. That's why the Bible says to give with a cheerful heart:

> *"But this I say: He who sows sparingly will also reap sparingly, and he who sows bountifully will also reap bountifully. So let each one give as he purposes in his heart, not grudgingly or of necessity; for **God loves a cheerful giver**. And God is able to make all grace abound*

toward you, that you, always having all sufficiency in all things, may have an abundance for every good work." (2 Corinthians 9:6-8)

God wants us to recognize He is the Lord of our finances. All we have we owe to Him, and we are simply worshiping Him by giving back to Him what is His anyway! When we give to God, we release Him to give back to us. The Bible says:

"Give and it will be given to you: good measure, pressed down, shaken together, running over will be put into your bosom. For with the same measure that you use, it will be measured back to you." (Luke 6:38)

Fellowship

First of all, it's a good idea to stay away from your old non-Christian buddies; not because you want to be a snob, but because they'll drag you down. For sure, they won't understand what's gotten into you. They'll be more likely to want to change your mind and make fun of your new-found belief in Jesus. Consider the basis of your past friendships. If you examine it, you'll find your old friends are drinking buddies, or people you "had fun" with. There's nothing wrong with having fun, but it all depends on the kind of "fun" you were looking for. At some point, you might be strong enough to talk to your friends about Christianity, but for now, it's best to stay away from friends who'll tempt you back into the old life.

One of the things you are looking for in a good church is Christian fellowship; like-minded Christians who you can be friends with, pray with, be accountable to, and learn from. So there are some guidelines to follow when looking for friends in church.

Look for people who will encourage you to righteousness, people who you can learn from, and of course people who are fun to be with. Make sure your new friends are committed to the

Lord, or they'll drag you down too. Just because people go to church doesn't mean they're good Christians. Your new friends need to be:

- committed and growing.

- unwilling to compromise with sin

- people you can confide in with your struggles and questions

- willing to be accountable to one another

- not ashamed to pray for one another.

When you are with other enthusiastic believers, it helps you see what God is doing in other people's lives, as well as your own. That can be very encouraging, because it builds your faith and shows you just how much God wants to be involved in each person's life. What He did to help one person grow or to answer another person's prayer, He will also do for you.

As we see people grow in the Lord, we see the wonder and beauty of God reflected in their lives. That is a very important principle of Godly living! When we are obedient to Him, He imparts a small part of Himself to us. God's whole plan for each of us is to make us more holy, more set apart for good works, more like Him! We are, after all, created in His image, and as Paul says, we are being *"transformed in the image of God from glory to glory"*. *(2 Corinthians 3:18)*

We are the Church!

Remember that you are the Church of Jesus Christ. The church is not a building or an institution; it is you and me. The Bible calls us the Body of Christ. Jesus said they will know you are His disciples by the love you have for one another. That love is the spark that ignites the Church! It is our lifeblood. As people look at us they see the reflection of Jesus in our lives.

If we are critical of one another, we are part of the problem, not the solution. If we practice love and forgiveness, the church becomes an awesome place, and we will draw others to the truth of Christ. Jesus wants us to practice unity as a testimony to the world that we are one as He and the Father are One.

Service

Now that you are part of the church family, you will want to become involved in some way. Every church has a need for people who will volunteer in the nursery, the children's Sunday School, as an usher, or just cleaning up in the sanctuary! None of these jobs needs a particular type of gift other than to be available to serve! Jesus said we are not to seek the leadership positions. But instead we should humble ourselves and try to serve one another.

"... whoever desires to become great among you, let him be your servant. And whoever desires to be first among you, let him be your slave; just as the Son of Man did not come to be served, but to serve, and to give His life a ransom for many." (Matthew 20:26-28)

Some people, once they learn the Christian lingo say such things as: "I don't feel called", if asked to help in some way. They are simply saying they don't want do something they think is beneath them.

But we are all called to serve. We are given special gifts by the Holy Spirit and they are all gifts that serve the rest of the church. <u>But the idea is to serve.</u> We don't need a "gift" to help clean up the sanctuary, or put away chairs! As Christians we should never say we won't serve. Too often 80% of the church do nothing, while all the work is done by 20%. When you join a church, find ways to help out in any way you can.

The Main points again..

After you've found your church...

- _____ at the church you've chosen.

- _____ for your Church.

- Become _____.

- _____ to your Church.

Fellowship: Your Christian friends need to be...

- committed and _____.

- unwilling to _____ with sin.

- people you can _____ in with your struggles and questions.

- willing to be _____ to one another.

- not _____ to pray for one another.

Service...

- How should you be involved in your church?

- Describe areas you think you could help out.

Action Point

How should you be involved in your church? Make a list of areas you think you could help out.

Also, describe in your own words your personal experience of the church you now attend. Are there ways you think they could be more friendly? Remember, this is now your church, and you have a responsibility to help it reach out to others. Your suggestions are valuable because you were once on the outside looking in!

Scriptures to Read and Memorize

Do not forsake the assembling of ourselves together, as is the manner of some, but exhort one another, and so much the more as you see the Day approaching.
(Hebrews 10:25)

But this I say: He who sows sparingly will also reap sparingly, and he who sows bountifully will also reap bountifully. So let each one give as he purposes in his heart, not grudgingly or of necessity; for God loves a cheerful giver. And God is able to make all grace abound toward you, that you, always having all sufficiency in all things, may have an abundance for every good work.
(2 Corinthians 9:6-8)

Therefore, as the elect of God, holy and beloved, put on tender mercies, kindness, humility, meekness, long-suffering; bearing with one another, and forgiving one another, if anyone has a complaint against another; even as Christ forgave you, so you also must do. But above all these things put on love, which is the bond of perfection. And let the peace of God rule in your hearts, to which also you were called in one body; and be thankful.
(Colossians 3:12-15)

... whoever desires to become great among you, let him be your servant. "And whoever desires to be first among you, let him be your slave; just as the Son of Man did not come to be served, but to serve, and to give His life a ransom for many. (Matthew 20:26-28)

~ Chapter Ten ~

Developing a Spiritual Lifestyle

Just because we have become Christians doesn't mean that all temptations leave and we suddenly live in this fantasy where everything is beautiful and nothing ever goes wrong. We find ourselves still getting upset, still drawn to the things of the world, in short, still committing sin. Do not despair! First of all God is very well aware of our human failings. He is not surprised or shocked that we sometimes fall into sin. The Bible says His mercies are everlasting:

"For as the heavens are high above the earth, so great is His mercy toward those who fear Him; as far as the east is from the west, so far has He removed our transgressions from us, as a father pities his children, so the LORD pities those who fear Him, for He knows our frame; He remembers that we are dust, as for man, his days are like grass; as a flower of the field, so he flourishes, for the wind passes over it, and it is gone, and its place remembers it no more, but the mercy of the LORD is from ever-

lasting to everlasting on those who fear Him, and His righteousness to children's children."(Psalms 103:11-18)

Resist Temptation

First of all, temptation is not sin. Sin only becomes sin when we entertain the thoughts that come into our mind. Even Jesus was tempted by Satan out in the wilderness, but He was able to resist the temptation. By the grace of God, you can resist too!

This means, when a temptation comes your way, you don't have to sin. I know you may be saying, "But you don't know how hard it is to resist!"

Wrong! There probably isn't anything you've thought about doing that I haven't thought about doing. That's because ever since Adam fell and disobeyed God, our hearts are drawn to the sinful side of life. The Bible says, *"There is none who does good, not one."* (Ps. 14:3) Sometimes, even when we think we're doing good, we can fool ourselves about our own motives!

"The heart is deceitful above all things, And desperately wicked; Who can know it?" (Jeremiah 17:9)

That's why it's laughable when people say we are at the pinnacle of evolution and will continue to get better and better. I don't know about you, but I don't see our humanistic lifestyle making things any better. More technology doesn't make us better; it simply makes it easier for us to spread our wickedness farther.

God is very aware of our sinful nature. He loves us anyway, because He knows what we were really created for, and sees that potential in all of us. When we become Christians, and the Holy Spirit comes to live with us, He gives us the power to overcome temptations. We are now new creatures in Christ, and we can resist temptation, with God's help, if we choose to. Sin is a choice and there are things we can do to make the right choice.

The first rule of resisting temptation is to avoid it! The Bible says flee! Flee immorality, flee youthful lusts, flee from idolatry.

'But you, O man of God, flee these things and pursue righteousness, godliness, faith, love, patience, gentleness. Fight the good fight of faith, lay hold on eternal life, to which you were also called and have confessed the good confession in the presence of many witnesses.'
(1 Timothy 6:11-12)

The bottom line is, don't go where you know you're going to be tempted. That's common sense, and doesn't really require a lot of spiritual power to do! Still, it's probably the most important piece of advice on how to avoid sin. Don't go there! Most people sin because they place themselves in a situation where they know there's danger. This is not only unwise, it's plain stupid. If you want to try to get as close to God as you can, what are you doing being in a place close to the devil's territory?

But if you do find yourself unavoidably in temptation, this is where the power of the Holy Spirit is there to help you. When you ask Him, he will give you the power to overcome any temptation. Here's what the Bible says:

"No temptation has overtaken you except such as is common to man; but God is faithful, who will not allow you to be tempted beyond what you are able, but with the temptation will also make the way of escape, that you may be able to bear it." (1 Corinthians 10:13)

That is the power of God to help you! If you ever run into temptation, turn right around, run away and call out to God, "Father help!!" He will give you the strength to resist.

But what happens if we do fall? And we know that we will fall, from time to time.

Confess

God simply wants us to come to him and confess it. In other words, agree with Him that we blew it. Just like any Father who loves His children, He is willing and eager to forgive us. That's what Jesus' sacrifice did for us! It allowed us to have immediate forgiveness as soon as we confess our sin to God and repent.

"If we confess our sins, He is faithful and just to forgive us our sins and to cleanse us from all unrighteousness." (1 John 1:9)

This is one of the great advantages we have as God's children. Every time we are forgiven, we get to start over! God forgets we have sinned and gives us a new slate. We know that God doesn't really "forget", but He chooses to act as if it never happened. He wants to forget! And we are blessed with a new beginning!

Repent

One of the words that we tend to ignore is the word "repent". Repent means to change our mind and therefore to move in the opposite direction. When Jesus declared the Kingdom of God, He told people to repent in order to partake of the kingdom.

Repentance is the key to the Christian life. It means that not only do we agree that what we have done is sinning against God (confession), but we intend to live our lives differently from now on. We *purpose* to do everything to avoid the occasion and opportunity for that sin.

Repentance means to **stop! Turn around! Go the other way!** And from now on we make a commitment to do everything we can to eliminate that sin from our lives. This is honoring to God. It pleases Him to see our willingness to obey Him. And He will intervene in our lives and enable us to overcome *"by His power"*.

The reason why most people never seem to have victory in their lives is *because they have not truly repented.* They want the blessings of Christianity, but don't want to make the effort to change themselves. This will result in very anemic Christianity at best. To be a true follower of Christ, we must repent and seek after righteousness with all our heart. Only then can we begin to have real victory in our lives.

Paul spoke about this kind of lifestyle when he talked about "putting to death the deeds of the body" (Romans 8:13). And not living according to our earthly desires. That way is death, and we will reap what we sow. We think we can get away with indulging ourselves, but that is not true! Sinful behavior will have its reward, just as righteous behavior has its own reward.

> *"Do not be deceived, God is not mocked; for whatever a man sows, that he will also reap. For he who sows to his flesh will of the flesh reap corruption, but he who sows to the Spirit will of the Spirit reap everlasting life.'* *(Galatians 6:7-9)*

Paul tells us that the process of denying the flesh is one that happens daily! (1 Corinthians 15:31) You don't just do it once and then its over! Temptations will be with us until we die. That's why we need to be in a constant state of confession and repentance before God. That's why we need to come to God daily.

But this is not a bad thing! Expressing to God our need for Him keeps us in a constant state of humility. And it keeps us open to promptings of the Holy Spirit and the blessings which he has for those who are obedient to him.

> *"Eye has not seen, nor ear heard, Nor have entered into the heart of man The things which God has prepared*

for those who love Him." But God has revealed them to us through His Spirit. For the Spirit searches all things, yes, the deep things of God. (1 Corinthians 2:9-10)

The Main Points Again...

- Now that we are Christians, are we free from sin?

- What should we do if we come up against a temptation?

- Are we able to resist the temptation? How?

- What should we do when we sin?

- How can we have victory in our daily lives?

Action Point

Write down your most difficult temptation. Describe how you become tempted to commit that particular sin. Do you see ways you could avoid the opportunity? Now select someone in the church who you trust and make yourself accountable to them. Ask them if you can confess your sin and receive prayer. When temptation comes, call the person you've chosen! This is your road to deliverance! Believe me, you'll see victory in time.

Scriptures to Read and Memorize

Flee also youthful lusts; but pursue righteousness, faith, love, peace with those who call on the Lord out of a pure heart. (2 Timothy 2:22)

No temptation has overtaken you except such as is common to man; but God is faithful, who will not allow you to be tempted beyond what you are able, but with the temptation will also make the way of escape, that you may be able to bear it. (1 Corinthians 10:13)

If we confess our sins, He is faithful and just to forgive us our sins and to cleanse us from all unrighteousness. (1 John 1:9)

Do not be deceived, God is not mocked; for whatever a man sows, that he will also reap. For he who sows to his flesh will of the flesh reap corruption, but he who sows to the Spirit will of the Spirit reap everlasting life. And let us not grow weary while doing good, for in due season we shall reap if we do not lose heart. (Galatians 6:7-9)

Chapter Eleven

You are Overcomers!

Victory Over Sin

If you talk to Christians who have a past of drug or alcohol abuse, you'll find a large percentage of them were able to overcome their habit because of the power of the Holy Spirit. While secular programs were unable to help them, God was. And that is the power that He has given to us to overcome sin, if we let Him. Too many Christians still walk in sinful habits and attitudes and claim they can't help themselves.

But that is not the gospel message! The message from Jesus is that you've been set free from the bondage of sin! You do have victory over sin! God says so.

"Reckon yourselves to be dead to sin but alive to God in Christ Jesus our Lord. Therefore do not let sin reign in your mortal body that you should obey its lusts." (Romans 6:11-12)

Jesus said,

"whoever commits sin is a slave of sin. and a slave does not stay in the house for long, but a son abides forever. If therefore the Son has set you free, you shall be free indeed." (John 8:34-36).

Therefore, you can have victory over every habit and addiction and sin in your life, if you surrender it to God. According to Jesus, you are a child of God. As a child of God, you have powers that can help you overcome your sinful self. The apostle Paul takes it for granted that you no longer need to live your life as you once did. You must make the choice to do that, but that's the least anyone can do!

"... put off, concerning your former conduct, the old man which grows corrupt according to the deceitful lusts, and be renewed in the spirit of your mind, and that you put on the new man which was created according to God, in true righteousness and holiness." (Ephesians 4:22-24)

Therefore, you have victory over sin! You do not need to be a slave to habitual sin in your life. Now that doesn't mean you never sin. We all still live in this fallen world and are prey to temptations all the time. But as we said in the previous chapter, God has equipped us to overcome any sin:

"God is faithful and will never allow us to be tempted beyond what we are able, but will with the temptation make a way of escape for us." (1 Corinthians 10:13)

That should be the greatest news any of us ever have! It doesn't necessarily make it easy for us to overcome the habits of a lifetime, but it does make it possible. Ask God now, for the ability to overcome the temptations of habitual sin. If you find it especially difficult to overcome sin, remember that the promises of God are totally true. Memorize scripture to use during difficult times.

Dealing With Strongholds

There may be spiritual strongholds in your life, from past habits or events. Strongholds are particular sins which you've indulged in over time. They may have become addictive behavior. Also, if you have been involved in occult practices, the devil may have a strong influence over you. Occult activity includes such things as using ouija boards, attending seances, using fortune tellers, involvement in witchcraft, spells and incantations. In short, any attempt to connect with the spirit realm other than through God.

Any dabbling in the occult is serious business! God calls it divination, because you are looking to demons when you should have been looking to Him. You've given the devil authority that should have been given to God. He will not easily let go of this authority! This may make it more difficult for you to overcome certain sins. But Jesus is far stronger than the devil or any demons. If you need to go to a friend or a leader in the church to help you, then do it! Your humility to seek for help in prayer will be honored by God. Remember that *"...greater is He that is in you (The Holy Spirit), than he that is in the world (the devil)." (1 John 4:4)* You are now Children of God! And God has given you all that you need to live a fulfilling and victorious Christian life!

The Secret to Victory is Surrender

You might have noticed that God's way is usually the opposite to the way the world seems to operate. For example, the Bible says the first shall be last. And if you want to be a leader in God's Kingdom, you must be the servant of all. Jesus tells us to love our enemies! God knows that the ways of the world eventually lead to destruction. The Bible said He has chosen, *"the foolish things of the world to put to shame the wise, and God has chosen the weak things of the world to put to shame the things which are mighty." (1 Corinthians 1:27)*

In the same way, if we want to live a victorious life, we must surrender! This is the secret to the Christian life: that we live constantly in a state of surrendering our will to God's. We can't break the habits of a lifetime in our own strength. We've allowed certain strongholds to enter our lives and take over. We must surrender it over to God, because He alone has the strength to defeat those strongholds and to give us a life of victory!

Before I was a Christian, I used to smoke a pack and a half of cigarettes a day. I had tried to quit countless times, but each time, my job, tensions, and simply the habits of a lifetime drew me back to my addiction. Finally, on the day I was baptized, I said to God, "Lord, you know I can't do this on my own. I need you to break the bondage. Please help me to quit!"

The next day, I was driving to work as always. And, as always, I reached for a cigarette. I was surprised to find out I didn't even want one! But I was skeptical. "Of course I want one," I thought to myself. "I'm just responding to some kind of autosuggestion!" So I reached into the glove compartment, pulled out a cigarette and lit up. When I inhaled, the taste of the tobacco was totally foul! I looked at the cigarette in surprise. Had God really given me a distaste for tobacco? I took another drag, and it tasted terrible! I put out the cigarette and never smoked again. I did not even go through withdrawal and I never craved a cigarette again.

Unfortunately, God doesn't always take away our bad habits quite so miraculously! Sometimes, He wants us to face our addictions and work with Him to eliminate our bad habits. For example, I had a terrible problem of swearing and He did not instantly deliver me from it! I had to deliberately focus on the problem of my foul mouth and stop myself from exploding with expletives!

Whether God removes the addiction sovereignly, or helps us as we work through it, the secret is to realize we can't do it ourselves! We need God to give us the victory, and in that way He is the one who gets the glory, because we know we could never do it on our own!

The Warmth of A Dynamic Love

One of the things which I hope you've been able to tell so far, is that God is not simply concerned with giving you tools to navigate your way through life. (Although He is certainly able to provide everything you need.) Whether you read between the lines of this book, or you read the lines themselves, you should realize **God is asking you to have a daily, ongoing, dynamic relationship with Him.**

When God created man, it was to share His love with His new creation. Then man fell, but God had also planned for this eventuality, and the gospel of Jesus came to fruition. It was the desire of our God to have this love relationship from the beginning. And we're not talking about a passive relationship. Obviously, if He has gone to all this trouble to help us along our way, He wishes more than a nodding acquaintance!

This is why he has given us tools of worship and prayer, to help us develop our spiritual senses and realize the extent of the blessing available to us through an ongoing walk with Him. Jesus constantly related to us how much the Father loves us. We are called his children. The apostle John tells us, *"Behold what manner of love the Father has bestowed on us, that we should be called children of God!" (1 John 3:1)*

The blessings of such a relationship should be obvious. If we live with the constant awareness of God's presence and love for us; if we strive to love and obey Him, to listen for His voice and promptings through the Holy Spirit (who we'll talk more about in the next chapter); if we practice the disciplines and overcoming principles which He has given to us, then we will live in the center of God's will, developing a vital love for Him, and experiencing His love for us in exciting ways!

Of course, such a relationship requires some effort on our

part, as in any partnership. Just as it's important for a married couple to work on their marriage, we too must make the effort to build on the foundation which God has provided for us. In Ephesians, chapter five, the apostle Paul even comments on the relationship between Jesus and the church (that's us, remember!) being very much the same as a marriage. And the more we develop our relationship with God, the more delightful and exciting it becomes! The honeymoon can continue for a lifetime.

That's what I mean by the "warmth of a dynamic love". If we abide with Him daily, as it talks about in John 15, then our love will never grow cold. We will never be far from the warmth of His love, and we will never feel distant from Him. In the midst of that kind of relationship, we are able to live without anxiety, as Paul says, when he urges us to rejoice in our life as children of God. He tells us,

"Be anxious for nothing, but in everything by prayer and supplication, with thanksgiving, let your requests be made known to God; and the peace of God, which surpasses all understanding, will guard your hearts and minds through Christ Jesus." (Philippians 4:6-7)

In this life, there are all kinds of things competing to take away our peace. There are opportunities for problems as far as the eye can see. We can have business issues, financial stresses, marriages and family relationships which could bring us down. But God has given us the tools to deal with all that. He can mend our broken relationships, restore our marriages, and give us contentment in our lives. All that, and we can rest in His love. A love, by the way, which will last for all eternity. Now that's eternal security, in the warmth of a dynamic love!

The Main Points Again...

- As a Christian, who are you now a slave to?

- What powers do we now have as an adopted child of God?

- Can we overcome habitual sin? How?

- What is the secret to victory over sin?

- Do you understand what it means to abide in "the warmth of His love"?

Action Points

If there are areas of occultic practices in your life, take the time now to write down what those activities were. Then pray and ask God to deliver you from any demonic stronghold which may be affecting your life. Renounce those past practices in Jesus' name. Then never look back. Christ has taken care of those areas, and washed them clean with the blood of His sacrifice.

Remember, don't try to conquer addictive sin with your own will power. You must surrender your will to the will of God, and allow His power to be used to overcome your sin!

Scriptures to Read and Memorize

Likewise you also, reckon yourselves to be dead indeed to sin, but alive to God in Christ Jesus our Lord. Therefore do not let sin reign in your mortal body, that you should obey it in its lusts. (Romans 6:11-12)

Jesus answered them, "Most assuredly, I say to you, whoever commits sin is a slave of sin. And a slave does not abide in the house forever, but a son abides forever. Therefore if the Son makes you free, you shall be free indeed. (John 8:34-36)

...put off, concerning your former conduct, the old man which grows corrupt according to the deceitful lusts, and be renewed in the spirit of your mind, and that you put on the new man which was created according to God, in true righteousness and holiness. (Ephesians 4:22-24)

You are of God, little children, and have overcome them, because He who is in you is greater than he who is in the world. (1 John 4:4)

~ Chapter Twelve ~

The Holy Spirit

Who is the Holy Spirit?

If you've been paying attention, you'll know that we spoke about the Holy Spirit earlier as the Third Person of the Trinity. As we said then, the word "trinity" simply means that God is One God, but consists of three distinct persons. There is no such word as trinity in the Bible, but it has been used to try and explain the relationship between the three persons of what is called the "Godhead".

There is no simple explanation of the way that God can be One in nature, yet also be three distinct persons. Many examples have been used to try to explain it, including St. Patrick's famous illustration of a three-leafed clover, which is one plant, but contains three leaves. Or the egg which consists of the white, the yolk and the shell. They all fall short of explaining the unexplainable. But just because we can't quite understand it, doesn't make it untrue! It's simply outside our ability to grasp.

There is no doubt that there is a third person of the Godhead known as the Holy Spirit. In fact He's a vital, active part in our lives every day. We know about the Father and the Son, because Jesus spoke of the Father while He was on earth. He also spoke about the Holy Spirit. He called Him the Comforter, or Helper, and said He has a special role to perform, after Jesus returned to the Father.

"And I will pray the Father, and He will give you another Helper, that He may abide with you forever; the Spirit of truth, whom the world cannot receive, because it neither sees Him nor knows Him; but you know Him, for He dwells with you and will be in you."(John 14:16-17)

Jesus also said the Holy Spirit would come and remind us of all the things which Jesus said.

"But the Helper, the Holy Spirit, whom the Father will send in My name, He will teach you all things, and bring to your remembrance all things that I said to you."(John 14:26)

The Holy Spirit has actually been active in your life since the beginning! The Bible says the Spirit leads us to knowledge of Him. And when you give your life to the Lord, the Holy Spirit comes and dwells within you, guiding you in all aspects of your new life.

"Do you not know that you are the temple of God and that the Spirit of God dwells in you?"(1 Corinthians 3:16)

It's the Holy Spirit who makes your Bible suddenly come alive! Or when you seek guidance in prayer, it is the Holy Spirit who directs you to the truth and the wisdom of a certain path. The Holy Spirit gives you the grace and the strength to overcome temptation, and to deal with the difficulties of your daily lives.

"However, when He, the Spirit of truth, has come, He will guide you into all truth; for He will not speak on His own authority, but whatever He hears He will speak; and He will tell you things to come." (John 16:13)

I believe the Holy Spirit is personal and specific in His guidance. There have been times in prayer when I know that God has given me a specific word of wisdom to speak, or a word of guidance in my own life. We do not live in a world of coincidences! When we listen for God's promptings, He speaks to us for our good! And God's Word confirms that this is true.

I remember very specifically asking God to give me guidance as to whether my family and I were to leave for a missions position on the island of Cyprus in the Mediterranean. Immediately after I prayed, I turned to my Bible as a source of help. I opened my Bible to the place where I was reading, and there in black and white were the words, *"Rise up and go to Cyprus...!"(Isaiah 23:12)*. Now if that's not a specific answer, I don't know what is!

Of course, I have to add, not every piece of direction which the Holy Spirit gives is that dramatic, or that specific. Nevertheless, it's a clear example of the fact that He is there to respond to our requests for wisdom, guidance or truth. In some fashion, the Holy Spirit will respond to us, because it is His delight to do so.

The Holy Spirit is also the one who imparts spiritual gifts to us. These are the gifts which we are given to minister to one another. When they are being used properly, they are an exciting part of God's plan.

Therefore I make known to you that no one speaking by the Spirit of God calls Jesus accursed, and no one can say that Jesus is Lord except by the Holy Spirit. There are diversities of gifts, but the same Spirit. There are differences of ministries, but the same Lord. And there are diversities of activities, but it is the same God who works all in all. But the manifestation of the Spirit is given to each one for the profit of all." (1 Corinthians 12:3-7)

What is Your Spiritual Gift?

The topic of Spiritual gifts is far too complex to get into in this short book. But it's important to know that God has provided each of us with special gifts from the Holy Spirit to help one another. We all have one or more of those gifts, and it's important to find out what they are. You can read about these gifts in 1 Corinthians 12-14, Romans 12, and Ephesians 4. These passages say that we have been given gifts to help and encourage one another. It also makes it clear that God made us to be a community that serves each other, or else why would He give us these gifts? They are certainly not for building ourselves up! They are designed for others, not ourselves. If people try to use these gifts to show how important they are, they have missed the whole point!

To find out more about Spiritual gifts and how they operate, search out one of the many good books available in Christian bookstores. Or ask your pastor what he would recommend.

The Controversial gifts.

One more point about what some have defined as the charismatic gifts of the Spirit. Ironically, the Holy Spirit of God, by Whom we are to be united as Christians, has been the subject of the most controversy. It is not our purpose to feed that division or even to participate in the debate. All we will say is that there is a Baptism of the Holy Spirit, because the Bible speaks about it.

"I indeed baptize you with water unto repentance, but He who is coming after me is mightier than I, whose

sandals I am not worthy to carry. He will baptize you with the Holy Spirit and fire." (Matthew 3:11)

Some churches say that the gift of tongues and other such manifestations of the Holy Spirit (words of wisdom, knowledge, miracles, tongues and interpretation, prophecy) are operating today and are an important aspect of Christian life. Other churches say some or all of these gifts stopped operating after the Bible was completed. Whatever is really the case we will find out in heaven. In the meantime, in an effort to maintain unity, we are not going to address those issues here. Please allow yourself to be led by the convictions of the pastors and spiritual leaders of your individual church.

As you become more familiar with the Bible, I would also encourage you to search the scriptures for yourself and make your own determination. The Lord wants us to read the Bible for ourselves and listen to the guidance of the Holy Spirit as He speaks to us about these, or any other matters. The people of Berea were complimented for their fair-mindedness because they listened to the Apostle Paul, and then *"...searched the Scriptures daily to find out whether these things were so." (Acts 17:11)*

As you study the scriptures about these gifts of the Spirit, simply remember the following two points:

1. Anything done to excess is not in Biblical order. All things are to be practiced decently and with proper order. (1 Corinthians 14: 39-40) God is not the author of chaos.

2. Whether a person does or does not practice the "charismatic" gifts does not make him or her a greater or lesser Christian in God's eyes. To God, we are all His children equally. That is why Paul focused on love as being the most important element of all in a Christian's life. (See 1 Corinthians 13)

The Main points again...

- Who is the Holy Spirit?

- What is His role?

- In what specific ways does He operate?

- What are the Gifts of the Spirit?

Action Point

Ask your pastor, or look for a book which describes the Spiritual Gifts and what they are. Take a spiritual gifts test, either by yourself or with a group. Once you find out what your gift or gifts are, find ways to express those gifts for the good of your church. Look up the Scriptures in 1 Corinthians 12-14, Romans 12 and Ephesians 4.

Scriptures to Read and Memorize.

And I will pray the Father, and He will give you another Helper, that He may abide with you forever; the Spirit of truth, whom the world cannot receive, because it neither sees Him nor knows Him; but you know Him, for He dwells with you and will be in you. (John 14:16-17)

But the Helper, the Holy Spirit, whom the Father will send in My name, He will teach you all things, and bring to your remembrance all things that I said to you. (John 14:26)

Do you not know that you are the temple of God and that the Spirit of God dwells in you? (1 Corinthians 3:16)

Therefore I make known to you that no one speaking by the Spirit of God calls Jesus accursed, and no one can say that Jesus is Lord except by the Holy Spirit. There are diversities of gifts, but the same Spirit. There are differences of ministries, but the same Lord. And there are diversities of activities, but it is the same God who works all in all. But the manifestation of the Spirit is given to each one for the profit of all. (1 Corinthians 12:3-7)

~ Chapter Thirteen ~

Your Role in Spiritual Warfare

You are in a Battle!

We have already spoken about the forces of darkness that are around us, taking every opportunity to tempt us and drag us back into captivity. You know about them if you've recently become a Christian, because you've been rescued from their domain! But you need to know that we're not talking about figures of speech here. The demonic world is very real, and Satan is a real person.

Satan is described as "Lucifer" in the Bible. (Isaiah 14:12) He is an angel, fallen from God's presence through his own pride. In the process, he took a third of the angels with him who rebelled against God's rule. These demons now expend all their efforts trying to destroy the Kingdom of God, and generally make our lives miserable!

These demon spirit beings tempt us to sin and follow their path of wickedness. But they are a pathetic lot because the Bible says they will eventually be cast into the lake of fire and be destroyed. They know this, because they read the Bible too! Still, they want to bring as many people as possible with them. As Christians, our job is to try and rescue people from hell. We do that by pointing them to salvation through faith in Jesus. As the Bible says, *"The wages of sin is death, but the gift of God is eternal life through Christ Jesus, Our Lord" (Romans 6:23)*

Jesus spent a large part of his ministry casting demons out of people. In fact, the Bible says that through his presence on earth and the work He did on the cross, Jesus was here to *"destroy the works of the devil." (1 John 3:8)*. So we can be sure there is a demonic presence and influence on this earth and impacting our lives. All we have to do is look at the world around us to see how well Satan has succeeded in dragging society to the brink of destruction. The battle is real and the stakes are people's eternal destiny!

We do not have to be afraid of the devil and his works, as long as we are believers in Jesus Christ. Jesus has given us authority over the devil. As a result, we too, can cast out demons and bring deliverance to people who need it, as long as we pray in the name and authority of Jesus. We also have the same authority to resist the devil's influence in our own lives. In fact, we are commanded to, *"resist the devil, and he will flee from you." (James 4:7)*.

The devil can only tempt us as long as we allow him. When we fall, it gives him delight, because he knows we are moving away from God, and towards his domain. The more we sin, the stronger a hold he has on us, until there arises a "stronghold" of sin in our lives. As we said earlier, a stronghold is an area of sin we can't seem to overcome. It happens because over time, we've given the devil authority in that area, or because we have engaged in occultic practices. But we do not have to be caught up in that stronghold! Jesus is stronger than any area of sin, and we can use His name and authority to break the strongholds of Satan.

As I mentioned before, if you feel there is an area of sin like that in your life, then go to other Christians and ask them to pray for you. Then take authority over the stronghold and break it's grip in Jesus' Name. You will receive deliverance, because God is far greater than anything the devil can do!

"You are of God, little children, and have overcome them, because He who is in you is greater than he who is in the world." (1 John 4:4)

You do not have to fear Satan, but you should respect him. He has caused a lot of misery and destruction in this world. And as Christians we should recognize his work and be on guard against his attacks. The Bible has given us the means to protect ourselves and take authority against Satan.

Finally, my brethren, be strong in the Lord and in the power of His might. Put on the whole armor of God, that you may be able to stand against the wiles of the devil. For we do not wrestle against flesh and blood, but against principalities, against powers, against the rulers of the darkness of this age, against spiritual hosts of wickedness in the heavenly places. Therefore take up the whole armor of God, that you may be able to withstand in the evil day, and having done all, to stand. (Ephesians 6:10-13)

As you read further into the book of Ephesians, you find that the armor consists of tools you already have at your disposal: the helmet of salvation, the shield of faith, the breastplate of righteousness, the sword of the Spirit, which is the word of God, the belt of truth, the shoes of the gospel, and prayer. All these things we have received through faith in Jesus Christ, or through the disciplines and study that we have spoken about here. Do not fear! As Jesus said, *"In this world, you will receive tribulation, but I have overcome the world..."*

The Main Points Again...

- Satan is described as _____ in the Bible.

- These demon spirit beings _____ us to _____.

- We do not have to be _____ of the devil and his _____

- The devil can only tempt us as long as we _____.

- The Bible has given us the _____ to protect ourselves and _____ against Satan.

Action Point

You don't have to look for demons in everything, but ask God to give you discernment, and you will see how the devil manipulates circumstances and people for his own ends. It would be a good idea for you to read more about Spiritual Warfare. At the least, read Ephesians 6, and see how God provides armor to protect us from the enemy.

Scriptures to Read and Memorize

He who sins is of the devil, for the devil has sinned from the beginning. For this purpose the Son of God was manifested, that He might destroy the works of the devil. (1 John 3:8)

Therefore submit to God. Resist the devil and he will flee from you. (James 4:7)

Finally, my brethren, be strong in the Lord and in the power of His might. put on the whole armor of God, that you may be able to stand against the wiles of the devil. For we do not wrestle against flesh and blood, but against principalities, against powers, against the rulers of the darkness of this age, against spiritual hosts of wickedness in the heavenly places. Therefore take up the whole armor of God, that you may be able to withstand in the evil day, and having done all, to stand. (Ephesians 6:10-13)

~ Chapter Fourteen ~

You are to Be Witnesses...

A critical job of the Church of Jesus Christ is to reach out to those who have not heard or understood the gospel. Jesus told us we are to be His witnesses. That means we tell people what He has done for us, so they can see the changes He's made in our lives. That's an important part of being a Christian. There is no other way people find out about the gospel. The apostle Peter said: *"Always be prepared to give an answer to everyone who asks you, to give the reason for the hope that you have". (1 Peter 3:15)*

Jesus has given us a mandate to "go into all the world". The command Jesus gave us in Matthew 28:18-20 is called the "Great Commission". This scripture is the foundation for the missionary movement in the church and is the reason why we send people around the world to spread the gospel. We are commanded to do this both around the world and in our own neighborhood.

I have heard many Christians, even ones who were supposedly mature, ask why we should support missions around the world when we have so many people in our own neighborhood who don't know God.

First of all, we have been commanded to go into the whole world, and we shouldn't ignore a direct order from our commander-in-chief! But I believe there are other compelling reasons.

We know that God works in the exact opposite to the ways of the world. Jesus said if you want to be great, then be the servant of all. Love your enemy. Give and you will receive. And I feel that, as we give our hearts and efforts to reaching people half way around the world, then God rewards our efforts by growth in our own back yard. I do know the most successful churches tend to be the ones most concerned about missions.

The other reason and the most important one to me, is that God's heart is for missions. Jesus Himself came to earth as a missionary to save us all. God has said that in heaven there will be people from every tongue and tribe. And He gave us the orders to get the job done.

I learned that in a very personal way myself about 15 years ago. Sandy and I had listened to a missionary who was working in a very needy part of the world. I listened to him and appreciated his efforts, but didn't feel like we were to help out. As we left the church that day, Sandy was speaking excitedly about the work the missionary was doing and then said, "Wouldn't it be exciting if we were supposed to go to the mission field?"

To tell you the truth, I wasn't very excited at the idea at all! I liked living where I was, and I didn't see any reason to go somewhere where I didn't know the language and the people might not like us! So I said to my wife, "Actually honey, I think we're called to stay right here."

She looked at me, and said "I don't think we should be so sure. How do you know God doesn't want us to go to the mission field?"

Well, I didn't know. But I did know that I wasn't ready in my own heart to go if God told us to. So, I had to stretch beyond my own plans and my own comfort zone to finally be able to say, "Okay God, we'll go, if you send us."

Sure enough, two years later we were making plans to move to Cyprus. From there we traveled and worked in many

Middle East countries, and even ended up living in Cairo, Egypt for a couple of years. As I look back on that now, God used that time to bless our family tremendously. He also used us to minister to a lot of people in the Middle East. I wouldn't have missed it for the world. But I almost did, because I was unwilling to hear God's heart for missions and placed my own desires first.

Missions is the heartbeat of God. He loves everyone in every nation, every tribe, every language. He wants everyone to come into His kingdom! (2 Peter 3:9)

You are a missionary, too

While not everyone is "called" to be a missionary, we are all able to be missionaries locally. This is not as intimidating as it sounds. There are many ways to do this. We can tell friends and family what we have experienced in our own lives. The greatest witness we have is what God is doing with us! But we should never try to shove the gospel down someone's throat! Just like you did, they will have to make up their own mind. You can invite them to church or a Bible study, but don't insist. Just make yourself available and allow them to see the transformation of God through your lives.

The other way we help with the Great Commission is to support local outreaches, missions programs and missionaries. You can support in prayer, financially, or you can go with a team on a local outreach yourself. In fact, one of the fastest ways to grow as a Christian is to go on a local outreach! You learn quickly how to pray, what to pray for, and how to rely on the Holy Spirit. When you are on an outreach of any kind, the only way it will succeed is if the Holy Spirit guides your plans and conversations.

Many people have never been on a local outreach because it's too far out of their comfort zones. Little do they know that's exactly where God wants them to be, because then God shows Himself to be faithful. When we are beyond our comfort zone, then we have to depend on God!

God wants you to be concerned about His people around the world. The hardest thing for most of us is to care about someone half a world away. But God has called us to be a part of reaching the lost wherever they are. When you join an outreach team, you will see that for yourself, because God shows you how much He cares for the least in the world's eyes. All are equal in God's sight! Everyone needs His salvation.

And so I urge you to become involved in some way with God's mission. You can do that by finding out what your church is doing in missions. Then pray and give to the missionaries which your church supports.

The Main Points Again...

- What is our role as witnesses of Christ?

- How can we be effective in telling others about the gospel?

- What is the "Great Commission"?

- Why should we support missionaries?

- How can we support missionaries?

Action Point

You can do several things to reach people in your neighborhood and around the world. Look for ways to be friendly to neighbors. Friends will be asking about your change of behavior. Have a good answer ready. Write it down, so you can be sure what you want to say. The Bible tells us to be ready to share our faith at any time.

Also, be on the lookout for a worthy missionary to support. They need your financial help and your prayers.

Ask God if He is calling you into a long term missions commitment. The fields are ripe and the workers are few...

Scriptures to Read and Memorize

But sanctify the Lord God in your hearts, and always be ready to give a defense to everyone who asks you a reason for the hope that is in you, with meekness and fear; (1 Peter 3:15)

And Jesus came and spoke to them, saying, "All authority has been given to Me in heaven and on earth. Go therefore and make disciples of all the nations, baptizing them in the name of the Father and of the Son and of the Holy Spirit, teaching them to observe all things that I have commanded you; and lo, I am with you always, even to the end of the age." Amen. (Matthew 28:18-20)

But you shall receive power when the Holy Spirit has come upon you; and you shall be witnesses to Me in Jerusalem, and in all Judea and Samaria, and to the end of the earth." (Acts 1:8)

~ Chapter Fifteen ~

He's Coming Again!

This is our fondest, most wonderful hope! We know that Jesus will return, as He promised, to take us up into His kingdom. We do not know when. Jesus said no man knows the hour or day. For this reason we are told to be on the alert!

"Therefore you also be ready, for the Son of Man is coming at an hour you do not expect." (Matthew 24:44)

Jesus told His disciples that He was going back to heaven to "prepare a place for us":

"In My Father's house are many mansions; if it were not so, I would have told you. I go to prepare a place for you. "And if I go and prepare a place for you, I will come again and receive you to Myself; that where I am, there you may be also." (John 14:2-3)

When Jesus ascended into heaven, his return was predicted by angels!

"And while they looked steadfastly toward heaven as

He went up, behold, two men stood by them in white apparel, who also said, "Men of Galilee, why do you stand gazing up into heaven? This same Jesus, who was taken up from you into heaven, will so come in like manner as you saw Him go into heaven." (Acts 1:10-11)

There has been much debate about whether Jesus is returning once or twice more. Some scholars say He will return first for his church who will be taken up to be with him in something called "the rapture".

"For the Lord Himself will descend from heaven with a shout, with the voice of an archangel, and with the trumpet of God. And the dead in Christ will rise first. Then we who are alive and remain shall be caught up together with them in the clouds to meet the Lord in the air. And thus we shall always be with the Lord." (1 Thessalonians 4:16-17)

Then he will return a second time to judge the earth and reign here for a thousand years.

"Immediately after the tribulation of those days the sun will be darkened, and the moon will not give its light; the stars will fall from heaven, and the powers of the heavens will be shaken. "Then the sign of the Son of Man will appear in heaven, and then all the tribes of the earth will mourn, and they will see the Son of Man coming on the clouds of heaven with power and great glory." (Matthew 24:29-30)

Blessed and holy is he who has part in the first resurrection. Over such the second death has no power, but they shall be priests of God and of Christ, and shall reign with Him a thousand years. (Revelation 20:6)

Not everyone agrees with this exact interpretation of how Christ will come, but all Bible believing Christians believe He is coming! Jesus Himself told us to be on the alert! He said, *"And behold, I am coming quickly, and My reward is with Me, to give to every one according to his work." (Revelation 22:12)*

Those of us who have become disciples of Jesus need never worry about His judgments. If we have believed that He died for our sins, then we know we will live forever with Him.

"These things I have written to you who believe in the name of the Son of God, that you may know that you have eternal life, and that you may continue to believe in the name of the Son of God.." (1 John 5:13)

One man was asked what his purpose in life was. His reply was direct and to the point. He said, "My purpose in life is to get to heaven, and to take as many people as I can with me!" If we examine that goal, we will see there can be no greater purpose for any of us. In the light of eternity, what else is there?

Jesus really *is* coming back soon! That is our great hope and wish. But in the light of that, how are we living our lives? When all is said and done, our small problems and trials mean nothing, compared to what God has in store for us. Let's live our lives as if each day will be the last. You never know; it might be! He may return today!

The Main Points Again...

What is the greatest hope of the Christian?

Do we know when this will happen?

What is the "rapture"?

Will there be signs that He is coming to reign on the earth?

Do we have to worry about the day of Judgment?

Action Point

Studying "end-times theology" can be fascinating. There are hundreds of books written speculating about when, where, who and how! There's even several fictional novels about it. About the only thing we know for sure is that nobody knows for sure! So have fun studying the prophecies and making your own guesses, but remember, if you're really sure you know, you don't! The only thing you can do to be ready for when Jesus comes is to expect him to come at any time, which is exactly what Jesus tells us to do. So be ready!

Scriptures to Read and Memorize.

"Therefore you also be ready, for the Son of Man is coming at an hour you do not expect. (Matthew 24:44)

"In My Father's house are many mansions; if it were not so, I would have told you. I go to prepare a place for you. And if I go and prepare a place for you, I will come again and receive you to Myself; that where I am, there you may be also." (John 14:2-3)

"For the Lord Himself will descend from heaven with a shout, with the voice of an archangel, and with the trumpet of God. And the dead in Christ will rise first. Then we who are alive and remain shall be caught up together with them in the clouds to meet the Lord in the air. And thus we shall always be with the Lord." (1 Thessalonians 4:16-17)

"These things I have written to you who believe in the name of the Son of God, that you may know that you have eternal life, and that you may continue to believe in the name of the Son of God."(1 John 5:13)

"And behold, I am coming quickly, and My reward is with Me, to give to every one according to his work." (Revelation 22:12)

Conclusion

It's been quite a few years since I gave my life to Christ in the living room in that house in British Columbia, Canada. Since then, Sandy and I have been halfway around the world and back. We have learned about the faithfulness of God first hand, and God has totally changed us.

Sandy and I reminded each other recently that if it weren't for God, our marriage would probably have hit the rocks long ago. But He made both of us totally new. I can't count the blessings He has heaped on us! We have a marriage that is full to the brim with love and contentment. Our children are all walking with God, we have friends all over the world and we know that none of it would have happened without the direct influence of God in our lives.

That doesn't mean there are no trials or disappointments. But we have the solid foundation of Jesus Christ to call upon in times of trouble. As the Bible says *"I can do all things through Christ who gives me strength." (Philippians 4:13)*

This foundation of faith and blessing does not happen naturally, just because you became a Christian. Many Christian lives have floundered on the rocks of tribulation, because they weren't prepared for the storms that would come their way. That's why Jesus spoke very clearly about some important conditions for the Christian life:

"Therefore whoever hears these sayings of Mine, and does them, I will liken him to a wise man who built his house on the rock: and the rain descended, the floods came, and the winds blew and beat on that house; and it did not fall, for it was founded on the rock. But everyone who hears these sayings of Mine, and does not do them, will be like a foolish man who built his house on the sand: and the rain descended, the floods came, and the winds blew and beat on that house; and it fell. And great was its fall." (Matthew 7:24-27)

The difference between the two foundations is that one man heard *and obeyed.* To hear and do nothing leads only to disaster. If we have learned anything over the years, it's to obey what God is saying to us, to the best of our knowledge. Every single adverse consequence happened in our lives as a result of stepping out without hearing the clear direction from God.

If you do the things we've mentioned in this book, you will have a head start on some people who've been Christians for years, but didn't hear or do these things right at the beginning. The Bible says *"don't be just hearers of the word, but be doers also." (James 1:22)*

Remember: the key is **obedience.** Find out what God wants you to do with your life and do it. Then hold on for the ride of your life, and on into the next!

Congratulations! You're well on your way. It's been a privilege to be a part of your life - to help you start your life with the Lord in the right way! May God bless you and keep you close to Him forever.